A History of
BEATTY,
NEVADA

A History of
BEATTY,
NEVADA

Robert D. McCracken

Nye County Press
TONOPAH   NEVADA

A History of Beatty, Nevada
by Robert D. McCracken

© Copyright 1992 by Nye County Press

Published in 1992 by Nye County Press
P.O. Box 3070
Tonopah, Nevada 89049

Library of Congress Catalog Card Number: 90-060812
ISBN: 1-878138-54-5

Design by Paul Cirac, White Sage Studios, Virginia City, Nevada
Printed in the United States of America

o the memory of Bob Montgomery and to all desert prospectors who dreamed of the big strike

n appreciation for their unwavering support and encouragement for the Nye County Town History Project:

Nye County Commissioners

Robert "Bobby" N. Revert
Joe S. Garcia, Jr.
Richard L. Carver
Barbara J. Raper
Dave Hannigan
Joe Maslach
Cameron McRae

and Nye County Planning Consultant
Stephen T. Bradhurst, Jr.

Contents

Preface

istorians generally consider the year 1890 as the close of the American frontier. By then, most of the western United States had been settled, ranches and farms developed, communities established, and roads and railroads constructed. The mining boomtowns, based on the lure of the overnight riches from newly developed lodes, were but a memory.

Although Nevada was granted statehood in 1864, examination of any map of the state from the late 1800s shows that although much of the state was mapped and its geographical features named, a vast region—stretching from Belmont south to the Las Vegas meadows, comprising most of Nye County—remained largely unsettled and unmapped. In 1890 most of southcentral Nevada remained very much a frontier, and it continued to be so for at least another twenty years.

The great mining booms at Tonopah (1900), Goldfield (1902), and Rhyolite/Beatty (1904) represent the last major flowerings of what might be called the Old West. Consequently, southcentral Nevada, notably Nye County—perhaps more than any other region of the West—remains close to the American frontier. In a real sense, a significant part of the frontier can still be found there. It exists in the attitudes, values, lifestyles, and memories of residents. The frontier-like character of the area is also visible in the relatively undisturbed condition of the natural environment, most of it essentially untouched by humans.

Aware of Nye County's close ties to our nation's frontier past and the scarcity of written sources on local history (especially after about 1920), the Nye County Board of Commissioners initiated the Nye County Town History Project (NCTHP) in 1987. The NCTHP is an effort to systematically collect and preserve the history of Nye County. The centerpiece of the NCTHP is a large set of interviews conducted with individuals who had knowledge of local history. The interviews provide a composite view of community and county history, revealing the flow of life and events for a part of Nevada that has heretofore been largely neglected by historians. Each interview was recorded, transcribed, and then edited lightly to preserve the language and speech patterns of those interviewed. All oral history interviews have been printed on acid-free paper and bound and archived in Nye County libraries, Special Collections in the James R. Dickinson Library at the University of Nevada, Las Vegas, and at other archival sites located throughout Nevada.

Collection of the oral histories has been accompanied by the assembling of a set of photographs depicting each community's history. These pictures have been obtained from participants in the oral history interviews and other present and past Nye County residents. Complete sets of these photographs have been archived along with the oral histories.

The oral histories and photo collections, as well as written sources, served as the basis for the preparation of this volume is situated on the southeastern margin of the Bullfrog Hills, a range of mountains of relatively modest height that is composed of tertiary volcanic materials, primarily rhyolite, with an aggregate thickness of at least 6000 feet. The highest point in the Bullfrog Hills, which would be called mountains anywhere else, is Sawtooth Mountain, which rises to an elevation of 6002 feet (Lincoln, 1923 [1982]:162); the Bullfrog Hills form the northern end of the Amargosa Valley and separate it from Sarcobatus Flat to the north. Beatty Mountain, which is treeless, lies to the immediate east of Beatty and rises to a height of 4282 feet. Bare Mountain, whose highest point is 6317 feet, takes its name from its bare, naked appearance (Carlson, 1974:46), lies just southeast of Beatty, and forms the northeastern margin of the Amargosa Valley. Bare Mountain is the site of a number of mines important to Beatty history, including Carrara and the Gold Ace on the west side and Crowells' fluorspar mine on the east. Yucca Mountain, an elongated and desolate-looking ridge of welded tuff, seemingly barren of vegetation, lies to the southeast of Bare Mountain and is visible from the Amargosa Valley. Beatty, with an elevation of 3309 feet, sits on a mile-wide flat at the extreme south end of Oasis Valley, sandwiched between the Bullfrog Hills on the west and Beatty Mountain on the east.

The Amargosa River, once described as a "feeble trickle," is the only stream of drinkable water within a radius of 40 miles (Ransome, 1907 [1983]:40–41). It originates from springs about 10 miles north of Beatty at Springdale and flows south down Oasis Valley through Beatty. It passes through the Beatty Narrows, located about one mile south of town, and enters the Amargosa Valley where it immediately sinks into underground channels. Then it flows southeastward down the Amargosa Valley, crosses the Nevada-California border, eventually turning northwest, to become lost in Death Valley (Carlson, 1974:36).

The Funeral and the Grapevine mountains, which form the eastern margin of Death Valley and the western margin of Amargosa Valley and Sarcobatus Flat, respectively, lie about 10 miles west of Beatty and are crossed at Daylight Pass (probably originally called Delight Pass [Palmer, 1948 [1980]:22]) by Highway 374. The old mining camp of Chloride Cliff is about 5 miles southeast of the Daylight Pass summit. Highway 267 crosses the Grapevine Mountains at Grapevine Canyon where Death Valley Scotty's Castle is located and then enters the northern end of Death Valley.

Other notable physiographic features of the region include the Spring Mountains massif, located about 60 miles to the southeast of Beatty, which rises to a height of 11,912 feet at Charleston Peak and which separates the Las Vegas Valley on the east and the Pahrump Valley on the west. The Panamint Range, whose highest point is Telescope Peak at 11,045 feet, forms the west side of Death Valley. The Panamints were the site of a number of prominent late nineteenth-century mining camps, including Panamint and Ballarat. (It is interesting to note that because the Panamint Range rises from below sea level out of Death Valley, Telescope Peak is actually "higher" than Mount Whitney [usually credited with being the highest mountain in the continental United States]. Although Mount Whitney is 14,494 feet, it rises from the Owens Valley, which is about 4000 feet in elevation. If we figure this way, Telescope Peak is "taller" than Mount Everest and is exceeded in the continental United States by a few of the volcanic peaks in the northwest, including Mount Rainier, near Seattle.)

Tolicha Peak (7058 feet), located about 25 miles north of Beatty; Timber Mountain (7421 feet), located east of Springdale; and Paiute Mesa, located east of Timber Mountain, are prominent physiographic features on restricted land belonging to the Nevada Test Site and the Nellis Air Force

Range. Stonewall Mountain (8318 feet), presumably named for Confederate General Thomas Jonathan "Stonewall" Jackson, is located on the northwest edge of Paiute Mesa about 17 miles south-southeast of Goldfield. About 25 miles west of Stonewall Mountain in the Lida area is Mount Magruder (9046 feet).

Beatty lies on the margin of the Mojave Desert (creosote) and Great Basin (sagebrush) ecosystems; it experiences four seasons, with relatively mild winters and hot summer days with cool nights. During all seasons, temperatures immediately north of the Beatty Narrows are noticeably lower than in the adjoining Amargosa Valley.

The majority of the principal mining communities in the Beatty area during its frontier boom period were located either in or on the margin of the Bullfrog Hills, and include, in addition to Beatty, Rhyolite (4 miles west of Beatty), Bullfrog (1 mile south of Rhyolite), Gold Center (just south of the Beatty Narrows), and Pioneer (5 miles north of Beatty). All except Beatty are now ghost towns.

The nearest modern settlement to Beatty is Amargosa Valley, a small community with a relatively dispersed population pattern, located primarily south of U.S. Highway 95 in the Amargosa Valley about 25 miles to the south; Las Vegas is 120 miles to the southeast. Goldfield is located about 65 miles north of Beatty on Highway 95; Tonopah is about 90 miles to the north. Furnace Creek, situated in the heart of Death Valley, is about 40 miles south of Beatty. Immediately east and north of Beatty lie the Nevada Test Site and the Nellis Air Force Range, the huge federal facility that occupies a large part of southern Nevada and is restricted to public access; Nellis and the Nevada Test Site are used for testing atomic weapons, aircraft, and other secret defense projects. Beatty has a small airport and no longer is served by railroad.

How Beatty Got Its Name

The town of Beatty is named after an early Oasis Valley resident, Montillus (Montillion) Murray "Old Man" Beatty. Beatty, a former Amargosa borax worker, was a native of Iowa and served with the Union in the Civil War. In the spring of 1896, Beatty moved into a previously occupied ranch just north of the present townsite and remained in the area until his death in December 1908. He was Beatty's first postmaster when the post office opened January 19, 1905, though he could neither read nor write, except for his name. Beatty, who said he had crossed Death Valley every month of the year, was married to a full-blooded Paiute woman from the Death Valley area; they had several children (Weight, 1972:13–17).

Early Residents of the Beatty Area

Archaeological evidence in Beatty and Oasis Valley is sparse; few sites that might provide significant information about early inhabitants have been found. It is not possible to precisely state when the first human beings entered the Beatty area. It seems likely that a culture of hunters and gatherers, known as the Clovis people, were in the area by 11,000 years ago. The Clovis culture is believed to have been based primarily on hunting, focusing on a number of species of large, now extinct, mammals, including the mammoth, camel, and giant sloth. The Clovis people are best known for a style of stone projectile point they made, which featured a fluted, or concave base. Because the fluted points have been found in many places in both North and South America, including the Las Vegas Valley, it is assumed the culture had an unusually wide dispersion. During this period, following the end of the earth's last glaciation period, the climate was cooler and wetter than it is today in Nevada. The dry lake beds that can now be seen in the valleys throughout Nevada are believed to have been filled with water and there was probably considerable vegetation near the lakes' margins. Humans and the animals on whom they subsisted likely congregated near the shorelines. The Clovis culture is believed to have lasted for several thousand years and disappeared when the climate became warmer and drier.

Although we can be fairly confident of human presence in the Beatty area about 11,000 years ago, some researchers now believe humans may have been in North America much earlier—more than 15,000 years ago or perhaps even as early as 30,000 years ago. It has been suggested that these pre-Clovis groups might have made their tools of bone and wood, which, unlike the stone projectile points of the Clovis culture, did not survive the millenniums of decay and thus have left few traces (Wolkomir, 1991). Again, although we cannot be certain, it is possible that pre-Clovis groups might have been in the Beatty area, either residing there or passing through on their way to some other place.

The first people to live in the Beatty area about whom we have more than scant information are the Western Shoshone. The Western Shoshone speak a language that is a part of the Numic branch of the Uto-Aztecan language family. (Uto-Aztecan is one of the largest language families in the New World, with speakers ranging from as far north as Idaho and as far south as Central America; it includes the language spoken by the Aztecs.) Members of the Numic branch include Mono, Northern Paiute, Shoshone, Comanche, Panamint, Southern Paiute, Ute, Chemehuevi, and Kawaiisu. The Numic languages of the Uto-Aztecan family are analogous in terms of close relationship to each other as the Romance languages are to the Indo-European language family, which includes French, Italian, and Spanish, with a high degree of similarity between words and grammars.

Although we know that the Western Shoshone have been in the central Nevada area for a very long time, researchers disagree about the length of time. On the basis of linguistic evidence, some researchers believe that ancestors of the Western Shoshone entered central Nevada about 1000 years ago from the Death Valley–southern California desert area, perhaps replacing or driving out the previous unknown occupants. Many archaeologists believe, however, that the ancestors of the Numic speakers are the descendants of the desert dwellers who resided in the area for many thousands of years, perhaps as far back as the Clovis people. Either way and measured by any standard, the Western Shoshone are long-term residents of the area (Charney, 1987).

The Western Shoshone in the Beatty area lived in an unusually harsh and barren environment; in some places the land was more barren than portions of Death Valley because the mountain ranges in the territory of the Beatty Indians were not as high as those in some adjoining areas and thus there was less moisture. It is estimated that in the latter half of the nineteenth century, the Indians in Beatty had a lower population density per square mile than most other Indian groups of the Great Basin (Steward, 1938 [1970]:48). The population density of Indians in the region of Beatty was 44 square miles per person in about 1875. In contrast, the population density at the same time was 2.1 square miles per person in the Owens Valley, 9.9 in Fish Lake Valley, 31 in the Belted Range, and 30 in Death Valley. Population density in Las Vegas and vicinity in 1872 was estimated at 28.5 square miles per person (Steward, 1938 [1970]:48–49).

Prior to the arrival of Europeans, the Western Shoshone practiced a hunting and gathering way of life. They lived as seminomads, moving within a defined geographical area where wild plants and game were available. Each family was, in all but a few activities, a self-sufficient economic unit. Tasks within each small group were divided according to gender. Women usually prepared the food, did the housekeeping, fashioned baskets and pottery, and made most of the family's clothing. They also collected seeds and other plant foods, although the men helped in collecting pine nuts. Men hunted, made stone tools and weapons, digging sticks and rabbit-skin blankets, and built their dwellings—conical-shaped huts consisting of a light frame covered with bark for winter use and a semicircular sunshade for summer (Steward, 1938 [1970]:44; Thomas et al., 1986:268).

In about 1875, there were six camps of Shoshone Indians in the immediate vicinity of Beatty; the camps were located along the Amargosa River in Oasis Valley and in the flat at the present site of Beatty. There were a total of 29 persons in four of these camps, and the other two camps were alternate sites. Numerous temporary camps were located at other watered sites in this area, which consisted of about 1300 square miles (Steward, 1938 [1970]:93–95). The Indians of the Beatty area frequently associated with other families of Western Shoshone living in the Belted Range across Paiute Mesa to the northeast and occasionally associated with other Shoshone in Death Valley and in the Kawich Mountains (Steward, 1938 [1970]:94). Warfare was unknown among the Beatty Indians (Steward, 1938 [1970]:98–99).

Scarcity of game in the area forced the Beatty Shoshone to subsist to "an unusual degree on vegetable foods." The early spring was often a difficult time for the Indians because the supply of seeds stored from the previous year was exhausted. During early spring, greens and Joshua tree bulbs were often taken from sites at Beatty Wash. In May and June, the women— and perhaps a few men—gathered sand bunch grass seeds at sites either 10 miles to the north of Beatty, on the southern side of Black Mountain, or in the vicinity of Big Dune and Calico Hills in the Amargosa Valley. After June, plants were gathered in the Beatty Wash, on Bare and Yucca mountains, and at sites in the Bullfrog Hills (Steward, 1938 [1970]:95–97).

In July, the Shoshone in the Beatty area moved to the southern portion of the Belted Range, where they gathered large grass seeds resembling wheat and, later in the summer, rye grass seeds. By August the seeds of most of the important food plants had ripened and fallen to the ground, so the families subsisted on rabbits, chuckwalla, rats, and other rodents and insects until the pine nuts were harvested. In late September and October, the pine nuts ripened and the Western Shoshone gathered this foodstuff. If the crop in the Belted Range was not good, they picked in the Grapevine Mountains. If neither site was productive, they went to the Kawich Mountains, 50 miles to the north, or to the vicinity of Lida. By 1860, corn, melons, pumpkins, sunflowers, beans, and perhaps other plants had been introduced into the area, but the Beatty Indians did not cultivate them on a large scale during this period (Steward, 1938 [1970]:95–97).

Animal foods were of secondary importance to the Indians in the Beatty area. There were few deer in their territory and antelope were either lacking or unimportant. Men often hunted mountain sheep in the Grapevine Mountains in early summer. Groups participated in communal rabbit drives with Indians from adjacent areas (Steward, 1938 [1970]:97–98).

Much is known about family and communal practices of the Western Shoshone. Marriages were arranged by the groom's father, who paid strings of bead money and a basket to the bride's father. The bride's mother, in turn, gave seeds to the groom's family. Marriages between blood relatives were forbidden. The use of strings of beads as money or as items of value may have predated the arrival of Caucasians in the area, but their main use was probably ornamental. Sweat houses were used by both men and women for smoking, gambling, and sweating.

Communal gatherings were infrequent and took place only when food was sufficient to provide for an unusually large number of people. The most significant communal gathering for the Shoshone, including the residents of the Beatty area, was the fall festival, which was held either at pine-nut picking time or in conjunction with the rabbit drive (Steward, 1938 [1970]:45–46). Residents from neighboring camps attended the five-day celebration. On the first night, an exhibition dance was performed by visitors from neighboring camps who were paid in bead money (Steward, 1938 [1970]:98). On the second through fifth nights, the Round Dance—the only Shoshone group ceremonial—was held. It was thought that the Round Dance would bring rain, crop fertility, and general well-being (Steward, 1938 [1970]:45). The dance was also performed for pleasure and offered an opportunity for courtship (Thomas et al. 1986:272). The groups dispersed at the end of the festival (Steward, 1938 [1970]:98).

Other rituals involved only individual families and were performed at the birth of a child, at the onset of female puberty (there were no puberty rites for boys), and at death (Steward, 1938 [1970]:45).

Beginning in the second half of the nineteenth century, incursions of Europeans and others into their territory began to disrupt the traditional way of life of the Western Shoshone in the Beatty area. The loss or damage of many traditional plant collection sites; reduction in game, garden areas, and camp sites; and the decimation of the already small population due to European diseases took their toll. Rather than live apart from the strangers who often occupied the most productive parts of their land, the Indians who did not perish from disease congregated around the settlements that sprang up in the area; they worked as laborers, ranch hands, and domestics. From the 1920s through the 1940s, a few ramshackle Indian dwellings were located in Beatty across the railroad tracks on both sides of the Amargosa River. After the 1940s, the residents dispersed to reservations at Walker Lake, Reese River, Duckwater, and other areas or were absorbed into Beatty itself (Hanes, 1982).

CHAPTER 2

Exploration and Settlement

ue to the inhospitable character of the region, the Beatty area was usually bypassed by the early explorers of the American West. Typically, early explorers followed seacoasts and lakefronts, rivers, and Indian trails when entering a new area. Attracted to verdant valleys and well-watered mountain ranges, which offered potential for abundance of wild game (especially beaver), they tended to follow naturally existing transportation corridors that minimized distances and were more likely to provide water, food for them and their animals, and shelter. The great barren region that was made of rugged mountain ranges, separated by dry desert valleys stretching for 100 or more miles in any direction from Beatty, offered none of these advantages. What Indian trails there were led only from one small water hole to another. Consequently, early explorers took more hospitable routes that led around the Beatty region. Entry into the vast desert area was justifiably viewed with considerable fear, holding the prospect of at least extreme hardship and perhaps even death, until well after the 1850s.

Ogden's 1829–1830 Expedition

It is possible that the famous Canadian explorer-trapper, Peter Skene Ogden, passed through the area where Beatty is now located on his 1829–1830 Snake Country Expedition, which originated in the Columbia River region, moved south to the Humboldt River in northern Nevada, and eventually "followed the eastern foothills of the Sierra southward to Walker Lake" (Cline, 1974:91). After leaving Walker Lake, Ogden passed through some highly inhospitable country, "traveling parallel to what is now the boundary between California and Nevada," perhaps passing through what is now the Nellis Air Force Range. On that passage, Ogden and his men experienced great hardships; they suffered from cold and hunger and went days without water. Their horses became weak and some died; the men were reduced to satisfying their hunger on the horses' carcasses and quenching their thirst on their blood (Cline, 1974: 93). Ogden's expedition eventually ended at the Gulf of California; he might have traveled through the Beatty area, perhaps moving south down Oasis Valley. Certainly the water sources in Oasis Valley would have made this route a possibility. If Ogden did pass through the Beatty area, he and his men would have been the first whites known to set foot there.

Fremont's Expeditions

On his second expedition (1843–1844), Colonel John C. Fremont returned to the East by way of the Old Spanish Trail; this route took him through the Pahrump Valley in southern Nye County and on to the Las Vegas Meadows in 1844 (Hulse, 1981:44). In 1845, on his third expedition, Fremont crossed the desert west of the Great Salt Lake and then split his party. One group followed the Humboldt River, while "Fremont and ten men crossed the Ruby Mountains, veering southward down the Big Smoky Valley and then northward to Walker Lake to rendezvous with the others" (Noren, 1982:7L). In 1848, Fremont published a map of the Great Basin, showing a grand "dividing range" running east and west across the Great Basin just north of the latitude of Beatty (Lingenfelter, 1986:37). Fremont claimed to have seen the mountain range from high points in the distance on his third expedition. This map with its imaginary mountain range was a major factor in the forty-niners' ill-fated decision to leave Captain Jefferson Hunt's wagon train on their way from Salt Lake to southern California; they then attempted to find a shortcut across the uncharted deserts of southcentral Nevada (Lingenfelter, 1986: 34). Though the forty-niners crossed the Amargosa Valley on their way to becoming "lost" in Death Valley, there is no evidence that any of the forty-niners entered Oasis Valley or the present site of Beatty prior to their descent into Death Valley in 1849.

On his fifth and last expedition (1853–1854), Colonel Fremont passed to the north of the Beatty area on his way to California. Fremont, who was looking for a suitable railroad route across the southwest, left Cedar City, Utah, in late February 1854 and struck out across the unexplored Escalante Desert. Fremont's party had had a difficult time in Utah, attempting to cross some of the most rugged country in the American West in the middle of one of the coldest winters the Mormons had experienced in their decade there (Egan, 1985:502). They "entered Nevada south of present-day Pioche and kept moving [passing north of Beatty] through a series of snowstorms until they reached the granite barrier of the Sierra Nevada at the thirty-seventh parallel, a little south of present-day Bishop, California" (Egan, 1985:503).

Early Settlers: Lander and Stockton

The Oasis Valley and the Beatty vicinity remained isolated and unsettled by whites until the 1870s. The discovery of a few mines in the area eventually resulted in the establishment of some small ranching operations.

Eugene Lander, a prospector from San Bernardino, is usually credited with being the first settler in the Beatty area. He was hard-working and industrious but never lucky; at least twice he was fairly close to the big bonanza, but he never struck it rich. Lander had two prospecting partners—August J. Franklin and a man named Hanson. High in the Funeral Mountains near Daylight Pass on the morning of August 13, 1871, Franklin spotted some promising float while he was killing a rattlesnake. (Float is a term for mineral-bearing rock that has broken free from an outcropping vein and rolled or been washed some distance from its spot of origin.) The next day, he and Hanson followed the float to its source on the crest of the range and found a great quartz belt laced with what they thought was silver chloride. Rough assays done in San Bernardino indicated the rock ran from $200 to $1000 a ton in silver. The three brought in friends as partners in the claim and formed the Chloride Cliff Mining Company. One of the friends, William M. Stockton, was an old partner of William Manly and Asabel Bennett of Death Valley forty-niner fame. They worked the ledge, which they named Chloride Cliff, until fall 1873. After they sank a 150-foot shaft, they took out over 100 tons of "ore" (Lingenfelter, 1986:136).

Soon they found that what they thought was silver chloride was really lead chloride, worth less than $28 a ton. The company folded in about 1873, but Franklin refused to believe that the mine would not pay; he worked it until his death in 1904. Franklin's son George continued to work the mine after his father's death and eventually sold it for $110,000. Ironically, the Chloride Cliff Mine was about 3 miles east of the Keane Wonder Mine, which produced $1 million in gold (Lingenfelter, 1986:136).

Lander quit the Chloride Cliff Mine but continued to prospect in the hills surrounding the upper Amargosa for nearly a decade. About 15 miles northeast of Chloride Cliff, across the Amargosa Valley on Bare Mountain (about 5 miles east and a little south of present-day Beatty), he found a large ledge of "black metal" in November 1879. He called it the Blue Monster in an area he named the Bromide mining district. The assays were said to run as high as $25,000 a ton and rumors had it that the legendary Lost Gunsight Lode had been found. (However, it was not possible that the Blue Monster could have been the Lost Gunsight Lode, for Jim Martin and some of the other Georgians among the forty-niners who found the rich silver ore were camping on the west side of Death Valley in a spur of the Panamints at the time of the Lost Gunsight's discovery. Bare Mountain is part of the second mountain range east of Death Valley.) William M. Stockton and others again joined to form a new company. They sunk several shafts and built a couple of arrastras. They even constructed a small furnace on the banks of the Amargosa to heat and extract the ore. But the ore came in pockets and was difficult to treat, and by 1886 most of the partners had given up. Just a few miles away the gold of the Bullfrog district waited to be discovered (Lingenfelter, 1986:136–137).

While Lander worked the pockety ores of the Blue Monster, he started a small ranch in 1879 in Oasis Valley, just north of the present site of Beatty. He stayed for a few years; when he moved on, his old partner William M. Stockton acquired the ranch September 22, 1882. Lander also held title to another ranch in Oasis Valley just 2 1/2 miles north of Stockton's (Brooks, 1970:41). Stockton used the ranch as a base of operations in his quest for the Lost Breyfogle and Lost Gunsight lodes (Lingenfelter, 1986:167).

In 1886, Thomas W. Brooks, a southern California resident, traveled from Los Angeles to Oasis Valley and wrote a series of newspaper articles about his journey. Brooks wrote of his arrival at Stockton's ranch in Oasis Valley and gives us a wonderful, detailed description of the terrain around the ranch.

> Early on the morning of the 14th we broke camp, and having but 15 miles to make to reach our point of destination, we arrived at noon. Having reached the headquarters of Mr. W. M. Stockton, who is the owner of a large, well-built, stone house and ranch, I made a brief investigation of my geographical whereabouts and of the general resources of the surrounding country.
>
> Mr. Stockton's ranch is situated two miles above the mouth of the canyon, on the northern border of the plains which we had just crossed, and in the lower southern end of the Oasis or upper valley of the Amargosa River, Nye County, Nevada. It is properly called Oasis (a fertile spot surrounded by barren waste or desert); innumerable springs of cold and hot water; a rich soil which will produce in large quantities any of the varieties of field or garden produce; and a never-failing meadow, densely covered with a good quality of grass.
>
> Of minor matters I may mention that on Mr. Stockton's ranch there are twelve large springs of fine water, which appear in a half circular shape in a cove to the east of the ranch and just at the foot of an abrupt, craggy mountain hanging over the twelve springs and at such elevation as to command a view of many miles of the valley. The immense projecting parts of the mountain and their peculiar shape so

excited my curiosity that I climbed the mountain to make an examination. Unacquainted with an easy and proper way to the cliffs, the route selected was difficult and hard, but I succeeded, and to my astonishment found them to be the dens—the homes—of many Indians, and that they had been frequented, possibly, for many thousands of years. From one to another I continued to climb and to search until I found thirteen immense [dens?] which could comfortably accommodate two or three hundred Indians. In some of these dens I found Indian stores, baskets, and broken crockery. The trail leading to these caverns was obscure and not visible from a natural point to ascend the mountain, but when found it was very distinct, and gave evidence of the great time it had been used. The solid rock was worn, not with the steel toed mule or horseshoes, but by sandals or human flesh—the bare feet of the aborigines.

The extreme headwater of the Amargosa River—the last sixteen miles of the valley to the north—is appropriately called Oasis. It is situated just across the line, in Nye County, Nevada. In this extent of country there are innumerable large springs of hot and cold water. Their temperature varies, as does the properties of the water, and no doubt there are springs, when known, that contain great virtues or medical values. Many of the springs have a temperature of blood heat, while in the valley others go above and below and as low as the temperature of cool drinking water, which proved to be of superior quality. I would mention that I saw a spring that flowed at least one thousand inches of water; and another of less quantity which, by an attempt to test its depth with a long rope with a stone attached to the end, was ascertained to be over fifty feet deep.

Of that part of the valley known as the Oasis there is about 1,300 acres of beautiful meadow land densely covered with good quality of grass. The quality of the meadow land is superb and is composed of disintegrated or decomposed lava and decayed vegetation and is black as jet. The country far and near surrounding the Oasis Valley abounds with a variety of interest. The country for many miles in all directions is extremely dry, hence the attractions of grass and water, and the mutual ground upon which various tribes of Indians have congregated for many centuries (Brooks, 1970:17–20).

Other Settlers in the Beatty Area

When Nye County Deputy Sheriff George Nicholl rode out from the county seat at Belmont in the spring of 1890 on an exploratory foray into the "southern country," as the southern region of the county was sometimes called at that time, he passed six unnamed valleys (Zanjani, 1988:48). Though 1890 marks the traditional end of the American frontier, the southern country was still largely unsettled. The few prospectors and settlers who lived in the area were a different breed; more often than not, they seemed to prefer to be alone or with Indians. Their backgrounds were often a mystery because it was not polite in desert society to ask a person where he came from or why he was there. In 1892, one writer suggested that some residents of the Death Valley area had come to escape the Civil War draft. Others, he noted, may have been deserters from the army or wanted for arrest in other areas. Some, he said, had come "for the same reason that the old sailors drank whiskey—because they liked it" (Spears, 1892 [1977]:55–56).

By 1890 George Lynch, George Davis and his family, John Howell, Jack Longstreet, and Montillus "Old Man" Beatty had settled in Oasis Valley. Not much is known about Lynch and Davis except that Lynch was not "at home" very much (Ritter, 1939 [1982]:1). In 1895 John Howell, the first known black resident of the Beatty area, tried his luck at ranching in Oasis Valley (Lingenfelter, 1986:168). Howell was no stranger at settling in the remote wilderness; with a partner, he had established the Spring Ranch at Las Vegas Springs as early as 1872 (Roske, 1986:38).

Andrew Jackson "Jack" Longstreet, a long-term resident of Nye County, was born in 1838, perhaps in Louisiana. Legend has it that Longstreet first showed up in the southern Nevada area in El Dorado on the Colorado River sometime prior to 1880 (Zanjani, 1988:12). He later owned a ranch in the Moapa Valley, and by 1890 had taken up a 160-acre homestead in the upper end of Oasis Valley. At that time he was one of three white men living in a 7000-square-mile area (Zanjani, 1988:48). Longstreet was said to have had five notches on his gun; and he wore long hair to cover his ears, both or one of which (sources differ) were said to have been cropped because of past indiscretions—perhaps horse thievery (Zanjani, 1988:12; 1987). Zanjani (1988:8) stated: "The men of Longstreet's day respected his extraordinary prowess with the long-barreled Colt .44 preferred by the old-time gunfighters, yet they distinguished him from that criminal underclass, often gamblers and sometimes thieves, to which many gunmen clearly belong. . . . Longstreet's killings were considered justified on grounds of self-defense." After leaving the Beatty area in the mid-1890s, Longstreet moved to Ash Meadows and later to sites in the Kawich and Monitor mountain ranges in northern Nye County.

"Old Man" Beatty (Montillus [Montillion] Murray Beatty), for whom Beatty is named, was a native of Iowa; he enlisted in the Union Army at Lyons, Iowa, on May 6, 1861, and served in Company I, Second Iowa Infantry Regiment (Weight, 1972:13). He was discharged because of disability and came west after the Civil War.

Beatty worked as a miner at Gold Mountain and in the Amargosa Valley. He acquired the Lander Ranch in spring 1896, not long after William Stockton's death. Beatty married a full-blooded Paiute woman and they had several children (Weight, 1972:13). He was described as a "generous, hard-working family man who made his ranch a welcome home to all who passed that way" (Lingenfelter, 1986:168).

Like many of his contemporaries in the area, Beatty chased tall tales of lost riches. There were legends that the forty-niners who had crossed the Amargosa were extremely wealthy and had buried as much as $200,000 in gold and jewels somewhere in the Amargosa Valley or Death Valley. When an Ash Meadows Paiute, Mary Scott, sold a prospector a solid gold watch that her father had found, it seemed proof of the legend. There were rumors that she also had a diamond bracelet and other fine jewelry. Prior to Beatty's acquisition of the Lander Ranch, he and Phi Lee searched for this treasure. They spent considerable time digging at old campsites, but found nothing except old wagon iron and broken china (Lingenfelter, 1986:171).

Beatty sold his ranch and its springs in 1906 to the Bullfrog Water, Power, and Light Company for $10,000 (Weight, 1972:13) and began a new ranch at Cow Creek in Death Valley. He continued to dabble in mining until his death in December 1908 (Lingenfelter, 1986:168).

The Beatty Area at the Turn of the Century

By early 1900, the area was still very much frontier. "Old Man" Beatty and his family occupied the stone house on his place at the lower end of Oasis Valley and John Howell was farther up the valley. Farther south there were a few settlers at Ash Meadows, with a couple of large ranches and a handful of smaller operations in both the Pahrump and Las Vegas valleys. There was a ranch at Indian Springs. More than 150 miles to the northeast as the crow flies, the mining town of Pioche, founded in the late 1860s, was past its prime as was Hiko, 100 miles from Beatty, at the north end of the Pahranagat Valley. A few ranchers were well established in the Pahranagat Valley. The first community east of Beatty that was more than a bar, a post office, and a one-room schoolhouse was Delamar, which was 50 miles south of Pioche. Belmont, 125 miles north of Beatty, was also past its prime and Tonopah's silver and Goldfield's gold had not yet been discovered. Across Death Valley, on the west side of the Panamints, the 1870s boom camp of Panamint had long since faded. The Harmony Borax Works in Death Valley were closed and the profitable days of mining playa borax had passed (Lingenfelter, 1986:186). A gold rush of some significance had begun in the last decade of the nineteenth century in the Death Valley area located to the west and south of Oasis Valley and the Bullfrog Hills. Gold had been found in the hills separating the Amargosa and Pahrump valleys in the 1890s and there were several gold camps in the Panamints, the most important of which was Ballarat, named after the famous Australian gold rush camp of the 1850s. Nearly 300 men were working in the Ballarat area by 1900 (Lingenfelter, 1986: 199–201). Miners and prospectors, always on the alert for new and better opportunities, left Ballarat nearly deserted when news of Jim Butler's discovery at Tonopah got around; the town never really recovered (Lingenfelter, 1986:200). The Tonopah discovery set off a rush of excitement and led to a boom in southern Nevada. People flocked to the area; prospectors took to the hills. Hopes rose at the thought of new discoveries of gold that might be made and the wealth that would inevitably come through investing in mining in America's last frontier, where, with a little luck, an average person could get rich quick. Ultimately, the prospectors took their pleasures in finding the riches the earth held; the promotors of the prospectors' discoveries would be right behind the prospectors, heralding the importance of the discoveries, often as not taking their pleasures in the mining of the pockets of investors as much as the deposits of gold and silver.

CHAPTER 3

The Boom Is On

here is a principle that governs all activity in the mining business. It might be called The First Law of Prospecting: You only find gold (or anything else for that matter) if you look for it. If you don't look, you don't find! The great twentieth-century boom camps at Tonopah, Goldfield, and Round Mountain were based on the discovery of precious metal deposits that literally stuck out of the ground. Native Americans had walked over the veins for millennia. Yet the black-stained stone at Tonopah and the gleaming flecks of gold in the rocks at Goldfield and Round Mountain had no meaning to the Indians; they weren't looking. The same can be said for the many travelers, ranchers, and outlaws who trekked over those outcroppings unaware of what fabulous treasures lay at their feet.

The gold in the green rock at Bullfrog had been there for millions of years; but it took the keen eye of an individual who could recognize what he saw to make the discovery. God put the gold at Bullfrog, but it wasn't for anybody to find. It took someone who knew about different types of rocks and the geologic formations and the indications of where gold might occur. It took someone who could survive on the desert with a burro, a blanket, a gold pan, and 30 miles by foot between water holes. It took someone who knew loneliness, a man of the desert, a true pioneer, a starry-eyed dreamer, a chaser of rainbows, perhaps even a fool, a ne'er-do-well by some city standards—a prospector.

The Montgomery Brothers: The Boom Begins

The Montgomery brothers, George, Frank, and Ernest Alexander (also known as Bob), started the great gold boom in the Death Valley area. They found the gold that opened the rush, they were behind the opening of the first big mines, and they stayed for more than twenty years until the boom was over. The Montgomery brothers were born in Canada and moved with their parents to a farm in Stuart, Iowa, after the Civil War. In 1884 they went west and worked in the mines in Wood River, Idaho (Lingenfelter, 1986:189). In late 1890, George was the first of the brothers to come to Death Valley; while looking for the Lost Breyfogle, he discovered the Chispa Mine (*chispa* is Spanish for "a nugget") about 50 miles southeast of the Bullfrog Hills in the Last Chance Range, which separates the Amargosa and Pahrump valleys. The discovery was one of several in the area. A few months later, about four miles to the north, the deposit at Johnnie was found by John Tecopa, the son of Chief Tecopa; and the Younts discovered the North Belle Mine a short distance away about the same time (Lingenfelter, 1986:18, 189–190).

In 1896 the Montgomery brothers discovered gold in the Panamint Mountains and named their claim the World Beater Mine. Eventually, the town of Ballarat was established nearby (Lingenfelter, 1986:194). In 1897 Bob Montgomery and a couple of partners made yet another discovery in a nearby canyon and they named it for their favorite whiskey: Oh Be Joyful (Lingenfelter, 1986:198). By 1900 Ballarat was the leading camp in the Panamints, with nearly 300 men working in the area mines (Lingenfelter, 1986:195, 199). But the discoveries at Tonopah in 1900 led to a mass exodus from the Panamints and Ballarat in 1901, and most of what was left of the town was destroyed by a flash flood that summer (Lingenfelter, 1986:200). In 1903 George Montgomery returned to Ballarat to restake his claim on the abandoned World Beater, which produced significant quantities of bullion before the high grade was exhausted in 1905. In 1905 discoveries at Bullfrog once again led to abandonment of Ballarat (Lingenfelter, 1986:202). Bob Montgomery left Ballarat and settled in Tonopah in 1901. He married and began to work as a jeweler and an optician; but his passion for gold was only temporarily cooled.

Shorty Harris and Ed Cross: "Lousy with Gold"

Frank "Shorty" Harris and Ernest "Ed" Cross are credited with the discovery on August 4, 1904, of "the fabulous gold-speckled green rock" found in the Bullfrog Hills a few miles southeast of what was to become the town of Rhyolite (Weight, 1972:3). Born in Rhode Island on July 21, 1857, Harris was orphaned at the age of seven. In the late 1870s he rode the rails west to seek his fortune in the mines. He searched in Leadville, Tombstone, the Coeur d'Alenes, and Death Valley. Harris, called Short Man by the local Indians (Caruthers, 1951:122), had a big, bushy mustache, blue eyes, big ears, and was barely 5'4" tall. He was known for his weakness for whiskey—the Oh Be Joyful. Cross has been described as a quiet, sober young newlywed (Lingenfelter, 1986:203). Shorty and Ed always disagreed about who really made the Bullfrog discovery. According to Shorty,

I didn't get in early enough at Tonopah and Goldfield, so
I wandered south and followed the Keane Wonder excitement in the Funeral range. I got there about as late as I did
elsewhere, so I didn't get any close-in ground. Long before
the Keane Wonder was struck, I had traveled across the
country from Grapevine to Buck Springs, and had seen the
big blowout of quartz and quartzite on the ground that later
I located as the Bullfrog claim. When I found that I couldn't
get anything good at the Keane Wonder, I remembered the
blowout and decided to go back to it. E. L. Cross was at the
Keane Wonder; he was there afoot.

"Shorty, I'd like to go with you," said Cross.

"Your chance is good," said I, "Come along!" (Ritter,
1939 [1982]:1–2).

In a 1930 interview for *Westways*, Shorty Harris described
what next happened:

So we left the Keane Wonder, went through Boundary
Canyon, and made camp at Buck Springs, five miles from a
ranch on the Amargosa where a squaw man by the name of
Monte Beatty lived. The next morning while Ed was cook-
ing, I went after the burros. They were feeding on the side of
a mountain near our camp, and about half a mile from the
spring. I carried my pick, as all prospectors do, even when
they are looking for their jacks—a man never knows just
when he is going to locate pay-ore. When I reached the
burros, they were right on the spot where the Bullfrog mine
was afterwards located. Two hundred feet away was a ledge
of rock with some copper stains on it. I walked over and
broke off a piece with my pick—and gosh, I couldn't believe
my own eyes. The chunks of gold were so big that I could see
them at arm's length—regular jewelry stone! In fact, a lot of
that ore was sent to jewelers in this country and England, and

they set it in rings, it was that pretty! Right then, it seemed to me that the whole mountain was gold.

I let out a yell, and Ed knew something had happened; so he came running up as fast as he could. When he got close enough to hear, I yelled again:

"Ed, we've got the world by the tail, or else we're coppered!"

We broke off several more pieces, and they were like the first—just lousy with gold. The rock was green, almost like turquoise, spotted with big chunks of yellow metal, and looked a lot like the back of a frog. This gave us an idea for naming our claim, so we called it the Bullfrog. The formation had a good dip, too. It looked like a real fissure vein; the kind that goes deep and has lots of real stuff in it. We hunted over that mountain for more outcroppings, but there were no others like the one the burros led me to. We had tumbled into the cream pitcher on the first one—so why waste time looking for skimmed milk?

That night we built a hot fire with greasewood, and melted the gold out of the specimens. We wanted to see how much was copper, and how much was the real stuff. And when the pan got red hot, and that gold ran out and formed a button, we knew that our strike was a big one, and that we were rich (Harris, 1930:18).

According to Shorty, the two waited until the next day to locate claims. Then they went over and showed the rich rock to Old Man Beatty, who immediately rushed over and located his own claim. George Davis heard about the strike and staked some ground for himself to the east. Harris and Cross told M. M. Detch, Len McGarry, and Bob Montgomery—the word quickly spread and the great Rhyolite boom was on (Ritter, 1939 [1982]:2).

In his version, Cross contended he was out digging and sampling one morning when he picked up a specimen about the size of a hen's egg that was heavy with gold. He said he took it back to camp, tested it, and then called Shorty (Weight, 1972:4). Most authorities credit Shorty with the discovery, however, if for no other reason than he seems to better fit the image of such a discoverer (Weight, 1972:3).

Montgomery "Re-infected" with Gold Fever

Montgomery, who was living in Tonopah at the time of Shorty and Ed's discovery, ran into Ed in Goldfield and was once again "mineralized"—a term the prospectors used to describe those infected by the gold bug. Shorty Harris described the scene:

> After the monuments were placed, we got some more rich samples, and went to the county seat to record our claim. Then we marched into Goldfield, and went to an eating-house. Ed finished his meal before I did, and went out into the street where he met Bob Montgomery, a miner that both of us knew. Ed showed him a sample of our ore, and Bob couldn't believe his eyes.
>
> "Where did you get that?" he asked.
>
> "Shorty and I found a ledge of it southwest of Bill [sic] Beatty's ranch," Ed told him.
>
> Bob thought he was having some fun with him and said so.
>
> "Oh, that's just a piece of float that you picked up somewhere. It's damn seldom ledges like that are found!"
>
> Just then I came walking up, and Ed said, "Ask Shorty if I ain't telling you the truth."
>
> "Bob," I said, "that's the biggest strike made since Goldfield was found. If you've got any sense at all, you'll go down

there as fast as you can, and get in on the ground floor!"

That seemed to be proof enough for him, and he went away in a hurry to get his outfit together—one horse and a cart to haul his tools and grub (Harris, 1930:19).

In September 1904, Montgomery headed for Bullfrog on a $75 grubstake by three Goldfield investors. He was unsuccessful and stayed only a few days.

On the way back to Goldfield, he stopped at John Howell's ranch in Oasis Valley (Lingenfelter, 1986:168, 207). There he met a young Shoshone known as Hungry Johnny, who claimed to know where ore could be found. Montgomery hired him to stake out two claims. Three weeks later, they met at Old Man Beatty's ranch and Hungry Johnny showed Montgomery the claims (Lingenfelter, 1986:207).

The claims, seemingly only a crumbly deposit of pink talc, did not look promising; but Montgomery took a chance and staked out two more adjoining claims—the Shoshone Nos. 2 and 3. The first assays ran less than $5 per ton. Montgomery took more samples and was still having no luck when, for an interest in the claims, a wizened old prospector named Al James agreed to show Montgomery where good gold values could be obtained on the Shoshone No. 3. Montgomery took samples in the talc where James designated and they ran $300 per ton in gold. An experienced miner, Montgomery wanted to get under the ore and cut it at depth and so a tunnel was driven below the deposit. He struck ore 70 feet thick that was assayed as high as $16,000 a ton (Lingenfelter, 1986:207). Tears filled Bob Montgomery's eyes when he first saw his new bonanza: "I have struck it; the thing that I have dreamed about since I was 15 years old has come true; I am fixed for life and nobody can take it away from me," he said (Lingenfelter, 1986:208). His find was heralded as "the greatest discovery ever made on the desert," "richer than the mines of King Solomon" (Lingenfelter, 1986:208). Montgomery's discovery and reports of fabulous assays from surrounding claims were ballyhooed nationwide (Lingenfelter, 1986:211).

Shorty Loses His Claim

After Harris and Cross made their discovery, they had assays run in Goldfield. The first showed $665 a ton in gold, and other samples reached $3000 (Lingenfelter, 1986:204). Once in Goldfield, Shorty characteristically headed for the saloons and the Oh Be Joyful. Cross quickly lined up a sale of their claims for $10,000, but the deal could not be completed because Shorty could not be found to close it. Shorty sobered up six days later, only to find that while he was in a drunken stupor he had sold his half of the claim for the low price of $1000, which he promptly spent on more drinks. Cross joined with J. W. McGalliard, who had purchased Shorty's portion of the claim, and together they formed a stock company, the Original Bullfrog Mines Syndicate. Cross eventually sold his interest in the syndicate to a San Francisco broker for a reported $125,000, and he and his wife used the money to buy a big ranch near Escondido (Lingenfelter, 1986:204).

Harris later gave this account of the disposal of his share of the Bullfrog claim.

> I woke up one morning and judging from the empties, I must have had a grand evening. I reached for a full pint on the table and under it was a piece of paper with a note. I read it and learned for the first time that I'd sold the Bullfrog (Caruthers, 1951:54).

Harris knew that the law would have released him from the contract, but as a man true to his word he declared, "I signed it." Years later he said, "At that, I got good money for a fellow like me," adding "I've never wanted for anything" (Caruthers, 1951:54–55).

> If I'd got those millions the big boys would have hauled me off to town, put a white shirt on me. Maybe they would have made me believe Shorty Harris was important. "Mr. Harris this and Mr. Harris that." I've got something they can't take away. I step out of my cabin every morning and look it over—100 miles of outdoors. All mine (Caruthers, 1951:55).

The Rhyolite Boom

Shorty Harris and Ed Cross were in Goldfield for only a few days. But word of their discovery in the Bullfrog Hills spread quickly. Goldfield and Tonopah were filled with "boomers," who had gotten to those towns too late to stake a valuable claim or in some other way to capitalize on the excitement. Most did not wait around for Shorty and Ed to head south to their claims; they gathered what information they could on the location and struck out on their own. Time was of the essence; a delay of a few hours, even a few minutes, could mean the difference between becoming rich and getting nothing. Shorty Harris described the scene he and Ed encountered when they arrived back at the site of their discovery:

> When Ed and I got back to our claim [Shorty speaks of the claim as his, but he had sold his interest.] a week later, more than a thousand men were camped around it, and they were coming in every day. A few had tents, but most of 'em were in open camps. One man had brought a wagonload of whiskey, pitched a tent, and made a bar by laying a plank across two barrels. He was serving the liquor in tincups, and doing a fine business.

That was the start of Rhyolite, and from then on things moved so fast that it made even us oldtimers dizzy. Men were swarming all over the mountains like ants, staking out claims, digging and blasting, and hurrying back to the county seat to record their holdings. There were extensions on all sides of our claim, and other claims covering the country in all directions.

In a few days, wagonloads of lumber began to arrive, and the first buildings were put up. These were called raghouses because they were half boards and half canvas. But this building material was so expensive that lots of men made dugouts, which didn't cost much more than plenty of sweat and blisters (Harris, 1930:19).

By September 1904, there were 75 men camped at Beatty's ranch alone. A returning Goldfielder met 52 outfits headed toward the new bonanza (Weight, 1972:7). "'What a procession!' the *Rhyolite Herald* recalled. 'Men on foot, burros, mule teams, freights, light rigs, saddle outfits, automobiles, houses on wheels—all coming down the line from Tonopah and Goldfield, raising a string of dust 100 miles long'" (Weight, 1972:7). R. A. Gibson, who was traveling from Chicago to Los Angeles by train, heard about the strike. He got off at Needles, gave the remainder of his ticket to a bum, and hired on as a swamper in order to reach the new bonanza. An 18-mule outfit belonging to H. D. and L. D. Porter, loaded with selected merchandise from their store in Randsburg, California, headed across Death Valley for Rhyolite in March and April 1905.

A covey of towns sprang up in the area adjoining the big strike. By mid-March 1905, Bullfrog had 20 tents and a population of 40; Amargosa, located 1 mile below Bullfrog, had 80 tents and a population of 160; Rhyolite had 100 tents and a population of 200; Bonanza had 1 tent; Gold Center had 20 tents; and the town of Beatty, the most propitiously located of all the communities in terms of the availability of water, had 150 tents and a population of 300 (Weight, 1972:7). Rhyolite, which lay in a horseshoe valley at the base of the mountains below Montgomery's Shoshone Mine, became the center of activity for the district; and the Shoshone became the "boss mine" of the Bullfrog district (Lingenfelter, 1986:209).

With characteristic hyperbole, Harris described Rhyolite's growth.

> Rhyolite grew like a mushroom. Gold Center was started four miles away, and Beatty's ranch became a town within a few months. There were 12,000 people in the three places, and two railroads were built out to Rhyolite. Shipments of gold were made every day, and some of the ore was so rich that it was sent by express with armed guards. And then a lot of cash came into Rhyolite—more than went out from the mines. It was this sucker money that put the town on the map quick. The stock exchange was doing a big business, and I remember that the price of Montgomery-Shoshone got up to ten dollars a share (Harris, 1930:19–20).

Senator William M. Stewart, a Comstock veteran and a renowned Nevada politician and mining lawyer, became a resident of Bullfrog (Weight, 1972:10). Senator Stewart owned an entire block on Main Street in Bullfrog, and his office and residence were the finest in the district. His office included a 1200-volume law library, said to be the best in the state (with the possible exception of the State Library at Carson City) (Weight, 1972:12). Stewart is quoted as saying, "If I had twenty grandsons I would plant them all in Bullfrog and let them grow up to be millionaires during the course of this present decade. . . . I look forward to seeing the early days of Cripple Creek and Goldfield duplicated." From the district, he said, "would arise in time the greatest camp the West has ever seen" (Weight, 1972:10).

But Bullfrog faded rapidly and by the end of May 1905, its population of 300 was eclipsed by Rhyolite's 1500 (Weight, 1972:10). There were 20 saloons operating in Rhyolite then (Weight, 1972:8). Initially, water was unavailable in Rhyolite and had to be hauled from Beatty by burro in whiskey barrels. The water tasted like whiskey and sold for $5 a barrel. In the summer of 1905, three rival companies completed pipelines from Beatty, Indian Springs, and Terry Springs to Rhyolite. Telephone service reached Rhyolite early in 1905. Electric power was first generated locally, then brought in from hydroelectric plants on Bishop Creek in California (Lingenfelter, 1986:222).

One week after completing a 270-mile trip overland from Caliente to Rhyolite via Goldfield with a freighter who did not know the direct route, Editor Earle R. Clemens brought out the first issue of the *Rhyolite Herald* on Friday, May 5, 1905 (Weight, 1972:7). A few weeks later, the *Herald* carried the following story.

> Rhyolite spread canvas faster than any town on the Nevada desert. Men scrambled to buy or lease the most favorable locations, regardless of price. The grocer, the baker, the booze dispenser . . . the druggist, the clothier, the hardware dealer, the newspaper man, the gambler, the hasher, the lodging house keeper, almost with one accord, hung out their signs and shingles. Within a few days every line of business and profession was represented and a full fledged community had been established.
>
> Concord Stages, drawn by fours and sixes, came daily from Goldfield, 75 miles on the north, and Las Vegas, 125 miles on the south. Automobiles by the score came from

Tonopah and Goldfield. From Goldfield stage fare was $18, auto $25. From Las Vegas the stage was $25, the trip took two days, one night. From Las Vegas freight took six to eight days, and dry camps had to be made.

The rainbow-chasers were crowded into canvas lodging houses partitioned with cheesecloth or burlap—proof against neither sight nor sound (Weight, 1972:8–10).

By 1907, the population of Rhyolite was 6000, making it the fourth largest town in Nevada, after Goldfield (estimated 20,000), Tonopah (estimated 10,000), and Reno (estimated 8,000) (Rocha, 1980:4). In 1907, 50 cars of freight were arriving daily on the Las Vegas and Tonopah Railroad. Lots in the heart of Rhyolite sold for $10,000 (Latschar, 1981:9). In January 1908, the John S. Cook & Co. Bank Building on Golden Street in Rhyolite was completed. The three-story building cost more than $90,000 and was constructed of concrete, steel, and glass, with Italian marble stairs, imported stained glass windows, and Honduran mahogany trim (Lingenfelter, 1986:219).

The boom, of course, was predicated upon the assumption that the hills around Rhyolite held valuable deposits of gold. The gold would be extracted by mining companies and there was the expectation of high profits, which would be reflected in stock prices. Such excitement led to the formation of more than 200 Bullfrog mining companies, which floated over 200 million shares of stock on the public. Most companies incorporated the name Bullfrog: Giant Bullfrog, Bullfrog Merger, Bullfrog Apex, Bullfrog Annex, Bullfrog Gold Dollar, Bullfrog Daisy, Bullfrog Starlight, Bullfrog Puritan, Bullfrog Outlaw, Bullfrog Mogul. Bob Montgomery and his partners formed a stock company, the Montgomery Shoshone Mine Company, in April 1905. Montgomery, who held three-quarters of the stock, boasted that he could take out $10,000 a day from his mine; the first shipment of ore was rumored to average $2300 a ton. There was talk of a big stamp mill to be constructed in Beatty, with a 3-mile aerial tram to the mine, but Montgomery's partners were already seeking a buyer. John W. Brock, the Philadelphia financier who had bought Jim Butler's mine in Tonopah, was approached, but his advisers cautioned him against the purchase because they thought the deposit was superficial (Lingenfelter, 1986:211–212).

In early 1906, Bob Montgomery sold his interest in the Montgomery Shoshone Mine to Charles Schwab, "the new saint of the American Dream of rags to riches, the epitome of upward mobility" (Lingenfelter, 1986:217). Schwab had risen from an engineer's helper at the age of eighteen to president and part owner of the Carnegie Steel Company at age thirty-five. Later, Schwab became president of U.S. Steel and was reportedly "the highest salaried man in the world," making over $2 million a year, with stock holdings in the tens of millions (Lingenfelter, 1986:216–217). Under Schwab's ownership nearly 2 miles of tunnels and drifts were developed at the Montgomery Shoshone Mine, and a mill that handled 300 tons per day was constructed at the mine, with water supplied by an 11-mile pipeline from Goss Spring. It was the biggest and most modern mill the Death Valley region had ever seen (Lingenfelter, 1986:218). Schwab arranged the mine's finances so that he would be paid back before any of the stockholders. Such an arrangement proved to be good foresight, for the mine's ore reserves proved to be neither deep nor extensive— the Montgomery Shoshone Mine was closed March 14, 1911. "The Montgomery Shoshone is dead," the *Rhyolite Herald* cried on March 25, 1911. Although the mine had produced $1,418,636.21 in bullion, it never paid a dividend. Its "profit" ($432,000) was partial repayment for Schwab's loans. When the mine closed, the mill and other machinery were sold to pay off the remaining $100,000 he was owed. Shareholder profits, it seemed, had gone "a glimmering" (Lingenfelter, 1986:239). It has been suggested that crushed ore at the Montgomery Shoshone mill suffered from "sliming"—forming such a fine material that metallurgical problems resulted in inadequate recovery of gold values in the ore (Hall, 1989:5).

Although Rhyolite experienced growth from 1904 to about 1907, the boom faded almost as quickly as it had appeared. The ore deposits, apparently lacking size and depth, simply could not long support a boomtown. Deposits might present good indications, but they quickly became exhausted. The Montgomery Shoshone mill continued to process low-grade ore, but there was nothing romantic about low-grade ore (Latschar, 1981:17). By disrupting financial markets, the San Francisco earthquake in 1906 slowed development (Latschar, 1981:9). The financial panic of 1907 affected other areas in Nevada and California more than it did Rhyolite (Latschar, 1981:12). In reality, the Rhyolite boom was predicated on speculation and could not be sustained. When news of shady dealings involving two of the district's most promising mines surfaced, investor confidence was eroded; and the March 1911 closure of the Montgomery Shoshone, the only mine in the district even to show significant production, was the final blow (Latschar, 1981:17).

One month later, on April 8, 1911, *Rhyolite Herald* Editor Clemens wrote (Weight, 1972:32): "It is with deep regret that I announce my retirement from the newspaper field in the Bullfrog district. It has been my lot to remain here while all my erstwhile contemporaries have fled, one by one, to more inviting localities, and now it is my time to say goodbye." Clemens went on to describe Rhyolite as "the prettiest, coziest mining town on the great American desert, a town blessed with ambitious, hopeful, courageous people, and with a cli-

mate second to none on earth. Goodbye, dear old Rhyolite."
George Probasco, who kept the newspaper going for another
month, wrote: "Rhyolite was about the biggest mining boom
and bust that ever happened. Until 1908, the sagebrush was
full of millionaires who a year or so later were wondering
about their next meal ticket or a free ride out of town" (Weight,
1972:32). Service to Rhyolite by the Las Vegas and Tonopah
Railroad was discontinued in 1914, and in 1916 the Nevada
Power Company cut off electricity (Latschar, 1981:19).

Most businesses had shut down or moved by 1911, and the
1920 census found only 14 residents. A 1922 motor tour of
Rhyolite by the *Los Angeles Times* found Rhyolite's only resident to be a 92-year-old man, who by 1924 had died (Hall,
1989:6).

Rhyolite's remains served mainly as a source of buildings
and building supplies to be scavenged for use in other towns
and camps. Many buildings were moved to Beatty: The Miners'
Union Hall became the Old Town Hall; one- and two-room
cabins were assembled into multi-room homes (Lisle, 1987);
and pieces of numerous buildings were used to construct a
school in Beatty. It is said some of the buildings eventually
ended up in Boulder City, Nevada, to house workers when
Hoover Dam was constructed in the early 1930s (Bradhurst,
1991). The desolate scene at Rhyolite was described by William Caruthers. Caruthers, a journalist who came to the Death
Valley area in 1926 and spent the next twenty-five years
observing life there, made a fire and camped in the empty
streets of Rhyolite on January 1, 1926.

> The next morning I poked around in the abandoned
> stores to marvel at the things of value left behind. China-
> ware and silver in hurriedly abandoned houses and in the

leading cafe. The cribs [one-room cabins used by prostitutes] still bore the castoff ribbons and silks of the girls and for all I know, the satin slipper which I found on a bed may have been the one that Shorty Harris filled with champagne to toast the charms of Flaming Jane" (Caruthers, 1951:55).

As the town's few remaining buildings decayed and ghosts of faded dreams took up residence among the ruins, Hollywood used the picturesque site as a film location. For a 1925 movie, Paramount Pictures restored the famous Bottle House, built of an estimated 50,000 bottles during the town's peak (Hall, 1989:6). Orion Pictures used Rhyolite's ruins as the setting for its 1987 science-fiction movie "Cherry 2000," which depicted American society in collapse.

Production figures for the great Tonopah, Goldfield, and Rhyolite-Bullfrog booms between the time of their discovery and 1920 are revealing (Elliott, 1966:311). Tonopah is credited with production of more than $109 million; Goldfield, $80 million; and Rhyolite-Bullfrog lags far behind with only about $1.8 million. Clearly, Rhyolite was based more on a dream of economic wealth than on reality—that harsh arbitrator of the fate of boomtowns.

Pioneer and Skidoo: The Last Hurrah

The presence of Pioneer, a short distance north of Rhyolite (2 miles west of the Springdale Station on the Bullfrog Goldfield Railroad), had arrested the decline of Rhyolite for a short time beginning in late 1908 (Latschar, 1981:17). The Bi-Metallic Mine, the chief producer at Pioneer, was the only mine in the area that came close to equaling the Montgomery Shoshone. The Bi-Metallic was purchased by Denver promoters in 1905. Later, a new company was formed, and in 1908 considerable rich ore was struck. Shipments from the Bi-Metallic Mine reached $60,000 a month in 1909, but before the end of July the mine became entangled in litigation and most of the town's residents left by the end of the summer. In early 1909, Pioneer's population reached about 2500, briefly surpassing the population of Rhyolite. The Western Federation of Miners, which had formed a local at Rhyolite, formed a new local at Pioneer. The community also had its own newspaper. Fire gutted the main business block of Pioneer on May 7, 1909, but the bank and red-light district were mercifully spared. The block was rebuilt by July 4, but by the end of the month the boom collapsed due to the tangle of litigation (Lingenfelter, 1986:230–233).

The last of the Death Valley gold boomtowns—Skidoo— was born in 1906. Bob Montgomery, who had become an instant millionaire when he sold his share of the Montgomery Shoshone Mine to Charles Schwab, continued to invest in mining. He purchased and developed 23 claims in the Panamints (Lingenfelter, 1986:286). His wife, Winnie (who purchased an alligator and pheasant farm in Mexico), named the area of the new claims Skidoo, after the popular phrase "23 skidoo" (Lingenfelter, 1986:216, 287). After the closure of the Keane Wonder Mine in the summer of 1916, "Bob Montgomery's Skidoo became the last survivor of the Death Valley gold boom" (Lingenfelter, 1986:307).

The rush to Skidoo began in May 1906. In July Montgomery laid out a town just north of the mine. He called the town Montgomery, but everybody else called it Skidoo and it was officially so designated on April Fool's Day, 1907 (Lingenfelter, 1986:289). The 56-mile road over Daylight Pass from Bullfrog to Skidoo was constructed in 1906 (Lingenfelter, 1986:290). The Skidoo Mine produced until September 1917 and yielded a total of $1,344,500 in gold, which made it the second largest producer in the Death Valley–Amargosa region. Its yield was just 5 percent short of the Montgomery Shoshone production total (Lingenfelter, 1986:308).

When Montgomery's final profit sheets were totaled, he ended up with a profit of less than 1 percent per annum over the period of the operation of the mine (Lingenfelter, 1986:308). By 1917 he had lost most of his money; none of his other mining ventures had panned out, and he also lost money in oil speculations in Mexico. He continued to speculate in mining for the remainder of his life and was working on a "deal" when he died on August 15, 1955, in Clovis, New Mexico, at the age of ninety-one. As Lingenfelter observed, the Death Valley gold boom lasted a quarter of a century; George Montgomery had been a part of its beginning at the Chispa Mine in 1890 and Bob Montgomery was there when it ended in 1917 (Lingenfelter, 1986:308–309).

A story in the *Bullfrog Miner* ("Sensation of the Mining World," May 12, 1906) captures the optimism—however fleeting—associated with most Nevada boomtowns.

> Just a few years ago it was Tonopah, Goldfield, and Bullfrog, in succession; a few months ago, it was Manhattan, Golddyke, Palmetto; a few weeks ago, comparatively, it was Fairview, Golden Arrow, Cueprite.
>
> A few days ago it was Buckskin that started a sensation.
>
> All the mining camps mentioned are in Nevada, but not all the mining camps in Nevada are mentioned.
>
> The mining camps of New Nevada are springing up like magic, and the best part of the story is that a remarkably large proportion of these camps is "making good."
>
> At least five of these mentioned have come to stay, and expert judgement is that either one of these five will

make it better than a Butte, or a Park City, or a Cripple Creek. . . .

Nevada, for the next few years, promises to be the sensation of the mining world.

When Gold Was Not Enough

Although prospectors were often singleminded in the pursuit of gold and wealth, they sometimes felt the need for companionship and love. But women were almost always in short supply in the Western frontier mining towns. The Beatty–Death Valley area was no exception—many of the prospectors and boomers were consigned to living alone. But that did not stop the Chaplinesque Shorty Harris from falling in love, though his objet d'amour was at least 8 inches taller than he was and probably outweighed him by more than 70 pounds. Harris tells of his ill-fated last attempt to marry.

I knew a girl in Ballarat by the name of Bessie Hart. She was a mighty fine woman and a good cook. No one in camp dared to pull any rough stuff around her—she was six feet tall, weighed 210 pounds, and could lick a husky man. I don't know why a little hammered-down fellow like me should fall in love with a woman like that—but I did just the same.

One day I was up by the Stone Corral sharpening picks in the blacksmith shop, and Bessie was blowing the bellows for me. Two of her best friends, Dean Harrison and Tom Walker, had gone to Tonopah, and she was missing them a lot, and I thought this would be a good chance for me.

"Miss Bessie," I said, "I guess you're kind of lonesome now since Dean and Tom are gone?"

"Oh, a little," she said.

"Well now, we've been kind of friendly for several

years, and since they aren't likely to come back, what's the matter with me and you getting married?"

She didn't say anything for a minute or two—just looked me over from head to foot—just gave me the top and bottom stuff, and I wondered if she was going to speak.

"Shorty," she said finally. "I like you.... You're a good friend and a handy little fellow to play with. But you're too little for hard work!"

That was all I needed to show me that I was out of luck when it came to getting a wife, and I've never tried since. ... But even if I've never been lucky at the game of love, I've had some good breaks when I was looking for gold (Harris, 1930:18).

Shorty was right. He never married, although he went on to make other discoveries of gold in the Death Valley area. However, he never became a wealthy man. Shorty Harris died November 10, 1934, and is buried in Death Valley. His epitaph is said to read: "Here lies Shorty Harris, a single blanket jackass prospector" (Weight, 1972:6).

CHAPTER 4

Beatty Beginnings

f all the communities established in the Bullfrog area, Beatty had the best location. The site was relatively flat, and water could be obtained from wells drilled in the center of town at depths of less than 30 feet (Weight, 1972:14). But the promotion, in spring 1905, of the new nearby townsite of Rhyolite, just west of the Montgomery Shoshone Mine, drew settlers from adjoining communities. The location of Rhyolite was a beautiful site for a town—a lovely desert valley surrounded on three sides by ridges of the Bullfrog Hills, open to the south, offering a wonderful view of the Funeral Mountains and the north end of the Amargosa Valley. Ladd Mountain was the high point on the east margin of the bowl in which Rhyolite sat; Sutherland Mountain was on the west; and Busch Peak was on the north. Rhyolite was high enough in the hills to be relatively cool in the summer, yet far enough south to experience mild winters. The valley was wide enough to accommodate a good-sized town, but the site had two drawbacks. It was a long way to water in any direction, and because the site was in a

bowl, open only on one end, it was not as accessible as Beatty.

Bob Montgomery Founds Beatty

If Bob Montgomery had not bought into the Beatty Township, it, too, might have become depopulated by the early exodus to Rhyolite. Montgomery's vow to build a grand hotel and make the town a milling center persuaded many Beatty residents not to join in the rush to Rhyolite (Lingenfelter, 1986:209). The town of Beatty was probably laid out in 1904 or 1905. Montgomery filed the first plat map of the community, which contains the names of Beatty's first streets. The post office was established January 19, 1905 (Carlson, 1974:48).

Montgomery himself hosted Beatty's first Thanksgiving dinner in a small tent on Main and Second Street in November 1904. Matt Hovek, Judge Sexton, J. R. McDonald, and Charles Watson were among the guests. The menu included bean soup, boiled beans and bacon, baked bacon and beans, desert flapjacks, and coffee (Weight, 1972:16).

Montgomery kept his promise to build a hotel in Beatty, and its construction probably played no small part in the consolidation of Beatty as a community. At a cost of $25,000, the hotel was the largest in the district at that time—indeed, one of the finest hotels in Nevada south of Reno. The grand opening of the Montgomery Hotel took place on October 25, 1905, with guests from as far away as Tonopah. A grand march was held, led by Mrs. Montgomery (who had come from San Francisco for the event) and Malcolm MacDonald, a Tonopah mining engineer and partner of Montgomery. Several weeks later Thanksgiving dinner was served at the establishment. The feast, elaborate by any standards (but especially in comparison to Montgomery's 1904 menu), included, among many other items, bluepoint oysters, chicken soup, Amargosa trout, lobster salad, potato salad, boiled chicken, calves' brains, roast young turkey, suckling pig, olives, pickles, green corn, stewed tomatoes, hot mince pie, pumpkin pie, New England plum pudding, hard and brandy sauce, nuts, cheese, Manhattan cocktails, a selection of wines, and cafe noir (Weight, 1972:16). (In 1909 the Montgomery Hotel was dismantled, moved to Pioneer, and renamed the Holland House; it later burned to the ground [Lingenfelter, 1986:231].)

In February 1906 (less than two years after he filed Beatty's plat map), Montgomery sold part of his Beatty interests, including the Montgomery Hotel, to Charles Schwab. But Schwab had no real interest in the Beatty holdings he had purchased from Montgomery, and shortly after the arrival of the Las Vegas and Tonopah Railroad, he sold them to Dr. William S. Phillips for a reported $100,000. Phillips, a con man known as the "little millionaire hustler from Chicago," proudly announced his plan to make Beatty the "Chicago of Nevada." When Beatty's second railroad, the Bullfrog Goldfield, arrived in 1907, Phillips flamboyantly revealed his design to build a $100,000 hotel, a hospital, a city hall, a church, and so forth. He placed signs on vacant lots around the town where he planned to construct these buildings. He sold as many lots as he could, then skipped town (Lingenfelter, 1986:229).

Bob Montgomery was thus the father of Beatty; and despite Schwab's lack of support for the town and Phillips' exploitative activities, the town survived its first years and was on its way to permanence on the Nevada map.

Newspapers in the Bullfrog District

The newspaper editor was usually an early arrival in a boom camp—not far behind the prospectors, boomers filing claims, saloon keepers, and good-time women. The local newspaper served as both a source of news as well as a self-appointed community booster, tirelessly extolling the virtues and bright future of the new camp. But the spirit of competition that infected early arrivals to the Bullfrog mining district for the most propitious sites to stake claims and build communities also engulfed the editors of the district's first two newspapers. A robust controversy quickly developed over who was entitled to use the name *Bullfrog Miner*. In early March 1905, C. W. Nicklin put out a sample edition of a paper called the *Bullfrog Miner* and mailed it to prospective subscribers (Lingenfelter and Gash, 1984:25). A few weeks later, he arrived in Beatty with press and materials, and on April 8 published the first regular edition. (Nicklin was "Johnny on the spot" when it came to starting a newspaper in a new town. On April 7, 1905, he started the *Las Vegas Age*, the third paper to start publication in Las Vegas within two weeks in anticipation that a bustling frontier community would spring up in the Las Vegas Valley and serve as a midway point on Senator William A. Clark's San Pedro, Los Angeles, and Salt Lake Railroad and as a supply center for the new mining towns to the north [Roske, 1986:144].) On March 31, 1905, Frank P. Mannix, at the urging of the Bullfrog Townsite Company, began publication in Bullfrog of a paper also named the *Bullfrog Miner*. Incessant quarreling followed over who had the rights to the catchy name. The word Bullfrog, of course, was magic in the district and both insisted on using it. There was also a superstition in the majority of western mining camps that working men would not accept a newspaper that did not have the word "miner" in the title (Lingenfelter and Gash, 1984:25). The quarrel continued until May when Nicklin renamed his paper the *Beatty Bullfrog Miner*.

The *Beatty Bullfrog Miner* changed hands several times; in May 1909, with Nicklin once again the owner, it was sold to Earle R. Clemens, owner of the *Rhyolite Herald*. Clyde R.

Terrell was owner or co-owner of the *Beatty Bullfrog Miner* between 1907 and 1909. Clemens folded the *Beatty Bullfrog Miner* in July 1909 (Lingenfelter and Gash, 1984:16).

When the town of Bullfrog lost out in competition with Rhyolite for population, Mannix moved the *Bullfrog Miner* to Rhyolite in spring 1906, where it was published in competition with the *Rhyolite Herald* until September 25, 1909, and then sold to the *Herald* (Lingenfelter and Gash, 1984:25, 218).

The most important paper in the Rhyolite district was the *Rhyolite Herald*, which began publication May 5, 1905, under the editorship of Earle R. Clemens. The *Herald* achieved a circulation of 10,000 by 1909 and was available on newsstands in Los Angeles, San Francisco, Salt Lake City, San Antonio, Omaha, Chicago, and New York. Clemens sold the paper in April 1911 and it ceased publication June 22, 1912 (Lingenfelter and Gash, 1984:16).

It would be nearly 35 years before the Beatty area would have another newspaper. On April 25, 1947, Robert A. Crandall began publishing a supplement to the *Goldfield News*, titled the *Beatty Bulletin*. It provided local news and was published until December 28, 1956, when the *Goldfield News* and *Tonopah Times-Bonanza* were merged (Lingenfelter and Gash, 1984:16).

Hauling Freight: Before the Railroads

The Bullfrog mining district was located in the middle of a vast little-explored wilderness, one of the most remote and inaccessible areas in the American West. Goldfield, the closest community of any consequence, was 65 miles to the north; Tonopah was about 90 miles away. Barren desert valleys separated by rugged mountain ranges lay to the east and west. One hundred and twenty miles of wilderness to the east separated Beatty and Pioche. To the west lay the Death Valley sink. More than 110 miles to the southeast was the Las Vegas Valley, where, like Beatty and Rhyolite, a new community called Las Vegas was beginning to develop. It was the beginning of the twentieth century, but as far as transportation and communication were concerned, it could have been the west 25 or even 50 years earlier. Until the railroads arrived in the Bullfrog district in late 1906, the only way to get in or out of the area was by horsepower or on foot, north to Goldfield or south to Las Vegas.

By the time Senator Clark's San Pedro, Los Angeles and Salt Lake (SP, LA, & SL) Railroad was completed in 1905, a rag town had developed on 80 acres of land located just north from Las Vegas's present downtown, which Canadian-born John T. Williams had purchased from Helen Stewart. On May 15, 1905, the railroad auctioned off subdivided lots at the Clark Townsite, located on either side of Fremont Street between Main and Fifth (Roske, 1986:55–56). The boom at Bullfrog and Rhyolite had provided an immediate spur to the Las Vegas economy, but not everyone who tried to make a success of a business venture made a profit. With the arrival of the railroad, many businesses engaged in forwarding freight delivered to Las Vegas on the railroad for shipment by wagon north prospered. By early June 1905, nearly 1500 horses were engaged in hauling freight from Las Vegas to Bullfrog, and 50 freighters would daily pass each other on the road (Paher, 1971:87).

Teams of 6, 12, 16, and 20 horses or mules were used. The large ensembles were driven with a "jerk line"—a single line attached to the lead animal. Roads were little more than a deep wagon track filled with a fine dust. A speedy rate of travel was 2 miles per hour. As they traveled, wagons and horses produced clouds of dust. A thick cast of dust formed on the faces of the drivers. At night, when the camp was made, the driver had to unhitch the team, feed and water the hungry animals, and dine on bread fried in bacon grease. At night he might be awakened several times by the unruly animals getting tangled up in the ropes. The next morning it was necessary to feed and water the animals, harness them, and once more begin a long day.

Though the opportunities for freighting goods and supplies north were ample, the business was not for beginners. William Thomas Stewart was one who tried and profited. Stewart, a Mormon, was born in Utah and had spent time in Delamar, the turn-of-the-century mining camp located southwest of Pioche in Lincoln County. Following the fading of Delamar, Stewart's family purchased a ranch in the Pahranagat Valley. Stewart's wife, however, did not like the unsettled character of the valley; she preferred Las Vegas, where she and her husband moved. Stewart, who was then employed as a carpenter, was highly skilled in working with horses. He jumped at the opportunity to purchase a six-horse team (known as a three-span) and two wagons owned by a Las Vegas physician who used the outfit to haul freight between Las Vegas and the Bullfrog district. The physician, like many in the freighting business at that time, had only limited understanding of horses and the subtleties of the freighting enterprise. Among other things, he was unable to hire teamsters, known as "skinners," who could or would "lay off the bottle," and he did not know the tricks of feeding and handling horses and loading wagons. As a result, the physician was losing money on the enterprise and offered to sell the three-span and two wagons to Stewart. Stewart purchased the outfit and immediately set about putting it on a paying basis.

The first thing Stewart did was to begin feeding the horses properly—plenty of oats along with their hay. With the improved diet, the horses put on weight and had more energy.

When he purchased them the horses had sores on their skin caused by the rubbing of ill-fitting collars and harnesses. Stewart treated the sores with ointment. He adjusted each horse's collar and harness so it fit properly and would not irritate the horse on the long drive. Moreover, he put the horses on a training program. Some of the horses (like some people) would not work hard without proper treatment and "incentives." The commands he gave the horses were always in a calm, firm voice. Stewart's son Dan, who ran cattle most of his life in the Groom Lake area and was also skilled in handling horses, states, "I've seen fellows that were balky drivers. They made their horses balky because they scream and holler at them, let them lunge and carry on. But my father, he knew how to handle livestock—he knew how to handle horses. He'd speak in a calm, gentle voice and just tell them to go" (Stewart, 1991).

Stewart's method for determining which horses were working and which were not was to hook them to a loaded wagon, set the brake, and speak to them in a calm and gentle voice, telling them to "move out." The horses that were working would "step right in and take hold," Stewart says. It was then obvious which horses were not pulling. Stewart would then say, "Whoa." If "one of them didn't get in and do his part," Stewart would step down off the wagon and "train him up with a halter chain"—whip them lightly on the ribs. A couple of sessions of that and "all he had to do was rattle the halter chain" (Stewart, 1991). In a short time, Stewart had his horses so well-fed and trained that the three-span was pulling 3000 pounds of freight per horse in the two wagons, an unusually large amount, on the Las Vegas—Bullfrog route. What is more, Stewart traveled alone. He had the same wagons, same horses, and same road conditions, but he made money where many others could not. The difference was in "the man on the seat," son Dan states (Stewart, 1991).

The trip to Bullfrog from Las Vegas took a week and Stewart could earn as much as $600 per round trip if everything went well. After leaving Las Vegas, he camped the first night at Tule Springs at the north end of the Las Vegas Valley; the second night was spent at Indian Springs. Water was available at both camps. The third night was spent at a dry camp between Indian Springs and Ash Meadows. The fourth night was at wet camp at Ash Meadows. The trip into Beatty took another two or three days; all those nights were spent at dry camps (Paher, 1971:95). He hauled groceries, mining equipment, and anything else that was needed in the boom camps. The freight, of course, came to Las Vegas on the railroad. Hay and grain were dropped off at all camps on the way north for use on the return to Las Vegas. A barrel of water was also deposited at dry camps for use on the way back. A teamster had little worry about the safety of feed and water—stealing a freighter's provisions could bring the death penalty to the thief on the Nevada desert.

The freighting to Bullfrog from Las Vegas by Stewart and the other skinners did not last long. At the end of December 1905 the first Las Vegas and Tonopah Railroad (LV&T) locomotive was delivered in Las Vegas for use in the first construction train on the railroad (Myrick, 1963:463). By March 1906 a train ran from Las Vegas to Indian Springs (Myrick, 1963:466), with full, regular service reaching Gold Center in October of that year (Myrick, 1963:475). As the railroad tracks moved north from Las Vegas, opportunities for freighters on the Las Vegas–Bullfrog route quickly evaporated in the face of competition from the iron horse. Following the establishment by the railroad of an autopassenger line between Las Vegas and Bullfrog, and completion of the Armor and Company ice and cold storage plant in Las Vegas in August 1905, meats, fruits and other perishables, in small quantities, were available in the Bullfrog district on a daily basis—although at a premium price (Paher, 1971:96).

Prudent person that he was, Stewart saved the profits he made from freighting and moved to the family ranch at Alamo, in the Pahranagat Valley. His wife was now willing to live there because it had become a little more developed while the family had been in Las Vegas. Interestingly, Stewart kept his wagons and horses upon returning to the Pahranagat Valley, and during World War I used them to haul rich lead ore from the Groom Mine on Bald Mountain in Lincoln County to the LV&T railhead at Indian Springs (Stewart, 1991).

The Railroads Reach Beatty

Of the three railroads that eventually connected in Beatty, the first to arrive was Senator William A. Clark's Las Vegas and Tonopah Railroad (LV&T). Clark had constructed the San Pedro, Los Angeles and Salt Lake Railroad (SP, LA, & SL) through Las Vegas, completing it in January 1905 (Myrick, 1963:455). Borax Smith planned a railroad that would connect Las Vegas with Tonopah, tying into Clark's railroad at Las Vegas (Myrick, 1963:461). When Clark refused to let Smith connect with his SP, LA, & SL, Smith abandoned plans for a Las Vegas destination and moved to Ludlow, California, where his Tonopah and Tidewater (T&T) line could connect with the Atchison, Topeka and Santa Fe. In October 1905 Clark purchased Smith's terminal site in Las Vegas along with 9 miles of completed grade to the north (Myrick, 1963:461). On Friday, October 12, 1906, the first regular passenger train made its run from Las Vegas to Gold Center, located about 5 miles south of Beatty, just beyond the Beatty Narrows (Myrick, 1963:475).

Fully scheduled service from Las Vegas to Beatty began on October 22, 1906, and Beatty celebrated by officially designating October 22 and 23 as Railroad Days. A delegation of local boosters traveled from Beatty to Las Vegas to meet special trains of celebrants from Salt Lake City and Los Angeles. The two special trains were combined into one, consisting of eleven Pullmans, a day coach, a diner, and two special cars of visiting dignitaries. Slowed by a breakdown on the desert, the delegation arrived in Beatty at 8:30 P.M. on October 22 (Myrick, 1963:475). The town was draped with festive bunting for the occasion, and visitors gathered at the Montgomery Hotel. After the celebration was over, one guest stated that the Railroad Days celebration "marked the camp's emancipation from the slavery of the desert" (Myrick, 1963:478).

The Beatty depot of the LV&T was located at the southeastern edge of town between Second Street and Third Street. The line's boardinghouse was constructed along the tracks to the north near the end of Second Street. The LV&T passed through Beatty to the north, circling first to Rhyolite, then on to Goldfield (Myrick, 1963:471). It ceased operations after twelve years, in October 1918 (Myrick, 1963:502).

The second railroad to reach Beatty was the Bullfrog Goldfield Railroad (BG), which arrived April 25, 1907 (Weight, 1972:17). It was financed by a syndicate that involved many prominent Philadelphians, including John Brock who had major mining holdings in Tonopah and had been behind construction of the Tonopah and Goldfield Railroad (Myrick, 1962:259; 1963:507). At Goldfield it connected with the Tonopah and Goldfield Railroad, which ran on to Tonopah (Myrick, 1963:505). South of Goldfield, stations included Keith, Stella, Cuprite, Wagner, San Carlos, Bonnie Claire, Jacksonville, Ancram, Springdale, Hot Springs, and Beatty (Myrick, 1963:505). The BG traveled south through Beatty, passed through the Beatty Narrows, and circled round the south end of the Bullfrog Hills to Rhyolite. After 1914, the Bullfrog Goldfield Railroad used the Las Vegas and Tonopah tracks from a point just south of Bonnie Claire to Goldfield, with the other tracks between Rhyolite and Goldfield being abandoned (Myrick, 1963:505).

The BG's arrival offered Beatty's citizens another opportunity for a celebration. A headline in the *Beatty Bullfrog Miner* read, "Railroad Day Beat Any Fourth of July We Ever Had." Excursion trains arrived from Los Angeles, Salt Lake City, Tonopah, and Goldfield. Old Man Beatty drove the symbolic golden spike uniting the rails, and more than 700 people banqueted in the Miners' Union Hall in Rhyolite (Weight, 1972:17). Although the Bullfrog Goldfield was a separate entity, it was dominated by the Las Vegas and Tonopah Railroad. The BG lasted until January 1928, when its last train departed from Beatty (Myrick, 1963:536). Because it duplicated service provided by the LV&T, Myrick (1963:505) called it, "Without a doubt, . . . Nevada's most unwanted railroad."

Borax Smith's Tonopah and Tidewater Railroad reached Beatty on October 27, 1907 (Carlson, 1974:48). Technically the T&T Railroad did not go into Beatty but went only as far as Gold Center; it then used the Bullfrog Goldfield's railroad tracks to travel on through the Beatty Narrows and into Beatty. All operations on the T&T ceased on June 14, 1940 (Myrick, 1963:593). On the fate of the T&T's materials, Myrick wrote:

> On July 18, 1942, contractors Sharp and Fellows began tearing up the rails at Beatty and, working southward, the job was completed all the way to Ludlow by July 25, 1943. Of the residue, a quantity of bridge timbers ended up as part of the Apple Valley Inn at Apple Valley, while the ties became scattered all over, a large number being used in the building

of the El Rancho Motel in Barstow. Two of the locomotives went to the Kaiser Steel Plant at Fontana, California, while a third went to the San Bernardino Air Base (Myrick, 1963:593).

Some old-timers in Beatty report that a T&T locomotive is buried under about 5 feet of dirt under Highway 95 just north of Beatty. In 1957 it was mired in the mud and crews upgrading the highway were in a hurry and simply covered it over with dirt rather than try to move it (Reidhead, 1987).

The Last Years of Old Man Beatty

Toward the end of his life—when he was more than 70 years old and when Beatty was just being platted, Old Man Beatty became the first postmaster in the town that bore his name. He was appointed despite the fact that he could not read and could write only his name, which he did with great care and in full. He assumed the post on January 19, 1905, and resigned March 24, 1906 (Weight, 1972:14–16). Two years later at the age of 73, Old Man Beatty died of a fall from a wagon while hauling wood from Bare Mountain. An editorial in the *Rhyolite Herald* eulogized him under the headline "The Last of the Squaw Men":

> Unlike many white men who lived with squaw wives, Old Man Beatty did not desert his companion when the country began to settle up. When fortune favored him, he gave his family all the comforts his fortune could afford. Whatever may have been the faults of this hearty pioneer, his devotion to his squaw and children evidenced a manly virtue. There is a genuine feeling of regret and a deep sense of loss among the oldtimers in the Bullfrog district over the death of this old man, whose cabin was a sheltering place for many a weary traveler in the early days, and whose hospitality was extended to the poor and rich alike (Weight, 1972:17).

Judge William Gray: Long-time Resident

Although many early residents of Beatty stayed for only short periods of time, one—Judge William Gray—was a resident from the time the town was founded until the World War II years. He made many contributions to the area. Judge Gray served for many years as the community's Justice of the Peace and also as land commissioner of the district. He helped build the church next door to his home in Beatty, and along with Walter Bond, constructed a road across Timber Mountain into Fortymile Canyon, now located on the Nevada Test Site. He helped secure Fortymile Canyon by locating placer claims along its bottom until Governor James G. Scrugham persuaded the Nevada legislature to set it aside as a state preserve. Fortymile Canyon was said to have been a "library of Indian writings." Gray also held mining claims in Skidoo (Lee, 1932:113).

Judge Gray was in Goldfield when the news of the Bullfrog discovery led to outlandish tales. He was initially impressed by the "boomers'" promotional activities in Goldfield and traveled south to see for himself. He was more than a little disappointed. "The boomers didn't care how much they told the truth," one old-timer later said. Boomers had put a display in a store window in Goldfield, featuring a chunk of gold as big as man's fist that was said to have been from the Kismet Mine high on Bare Mountain; next to it was a big trout. A sign in the window read: "Come to Gold Center. Find mines with ore like this. Catch trout like this one in the Amargosa River." In Goldfield, boomers showed Gray lithographs of the Amargosa River with boats on it. In the pictures, the river's banks were lined with trees and cattle grazed in lush green pastures. In contrast old-timers in Beatty often swore that they had seen fish in the Amargosa River carrying patched canteens (Lee, 1932:114).

J. Irving Crowell and the Chloride Cliff Mine

J. Irving Crowell arrived in Beatty in 1905 after a three-day trip by horse and buggy from Las Vegas. He was originally from New England and had been raised on Cape Cod. His wife, Annie, a Canadian, remained in the couple's home in Los Angeles while Crowell was on the desert seeking his fortune as a mining promoter (J. I. and D. Crowell, 1987).

The Chloride Cliff Mine, located near the crest of the Funeral Mountains almost due west of Beatty and south of Daylight Pass, was an old mine; it had originally been discovered by August J. Franklin, a man named Hanson, and Beatty pioneer Eugene Lander in August 1871. The company Franklin and his partners formed was disbanded, but Franklin continued to hold the property until his death in 1904, when his son George took it over. Activity at the nearby Keane Wonder Mine led to revived interest in the immediate area, and prior to the Panic of 1907, J. Irving Crowell purchased an interest in the Chloride Cliff Mine from George Franklin for an estimated $110,000 (Lingenfelter, 1986:136).

After his initial purchase, Crowell obtained backing from investors in Pennsylvania and reopened the mine under the banner of the Penn Mining and Leasing Company in the fall of 1909. Crowell found gold-bearing rock assaying at better than $35 a ton and constructed a 1-stamp mill at the foot of the mine dump. Some ore was shipped, and at one point Crowell attempted unsuccessfully to sell his holdings to investors in England (Lingenfelter, 1986:304–305). Crowell maintained a residence on the property until 1917 (J. I. and D. Crowell, 1987). Crowell's son, J. Irving Crowell, Jr., said that his father never made a lot of money on the Chloride Cliff Mine but that some leasers did fairly well (J. and M-K. Crowell, 1987).

J. Irving, Jr., was born in Los Angeles in 1900. He attended public schools in Los Angeles, and as a youth spent his summers with his father at Chloride Cliff. Young Crowell first came to Rhyolite in 1910 and stayed at the Southern Hotel, where he had his first taste of champagne. Crowell, Jr., recalled little activity in Beatty during this period; most of the action was in Rhyolite. "In 1917," Crowell said, "Beatty was a shell of what it is now." He remembered traveling to Gold Center with his father around 1912 to look at a mill. Rather than walk back to Beatty they flagged down the LV&T by standing in the middle of the tracks and waving their shirts. The engineer acknowledged them by blowing his whistle twice, slowed down, and stopped in front of them (J. I. and D. Crowell, 1987).

The Chloride Cliff Mine was 18 miles from Rhyolite; the trip took 5 hours by horse and buggy. Sometimes young Crowell would accompany his father into Rhyolite for supplies, and the father and son would spend the night in Rhyolite and return the next day. Al McPherson, a teamster in Beatty, often hauled supplies from Rhyolite out to the Chloride Cliff. Crowell had no phone at his place, but there was one at the nearby Keane Wonder Mine. Sometimes the elder Crowell would walk to the Keane Wonder and call an order in to McPherson, who would then bring it out (J. I. and D. Crowell, 1987).

The Crowells' Fluorspar Mine

In 1917 a man named Bill Kennedy was prospecting on Bare Mountain. He threw down his pick and broke loose a piece of soft, purple rock. The next day he happened to meet J. I. Crowell and showed him a specimen. Crowell recognized the sample as fluorspar (calcium fluoride), and he purchased the information on the formation's location for $500 cash. Following Kennedy's directions, Crowell went to the site, staked out a claim, and filed a location notice. He named his new claim the Daisy. Over the years several other claims were added to what is now sometimes referred to as the Daisy Group (J. I. and D. Crowell, 1987).

Originally Crowell's interest in the Daisy focused on gold prospects rather than fluorspar, the presence of which was believed to be a favorable indication that gold-bearing ore existed at lower levels. Fluorspar was much less glamorous than gold and was used primarily as a catalyst in the production of steel; it has the effect of making molten slag thinner and more fluid. Although Crowell never found gold at his fluorspar mine, the property has proven to be a solid producer of fluorspar; it was the longest continuously operated mine in the Beatty–Death Valley area (J. I. and D. Crowell, 1987).

Shortly after filing on his fluorspar claim, Crowell moved from Chloride Cliff to Beatty. Louis Vidano, who had worked with Crowell at the Chloride Cliff Mine for several years, accompanied him to his new mining property on Bare Mountain. They began sinking a shaft in the fluorspar; the material was so soft that holes for blasting could be drilled with a hand auger. A headframe was built, and ore was hoisted with a 15-horsepower Fairbanks-Morse torch-ignited engine. Crowell worked the mine steadily until 1923, at which time the shaft was 134 feet deep. In the early 1920s Crowell attempted to concentrate the fluorspar ore in a mill constructed behind his home in Beatty. The fluorspar was originally run over gravity tables; later a flotation process was used. The efforts did not last long, however, and no milling has been done at the site since. Instead, the ore was handsorted to remove the waste rock. The fluorspar ore shipped from the mine was known as 85/5 ore, meaning it contained a minimum of 85 percent calcium fluoride and less than 5 percent silica (J. I. and D. Crowell, 1987).

In 1923, personal misfortune struck Crowell. For years he made regular visits to his wife and family in Los Angeles by boarding a Pullman in Beatty and traveling down the T&T to Ludlow, where the car was transferred to the Santa Fe Railroad tracks for the ride to Los Angeles. On one fateful trip, when the Pullman was transferred to the Santa Fe the train did not hook properly onto the Pullman, and the car came loose. The Santa Fe train backed up to connect the Pullman, which by this time stood motionless on the tracks. The engineer misjudged the distance between the train and the stray car and rammed the Pullman at 35 miles an hour. Crowell was thrown head-first through a partition and was severely injured. He was an invalid for months. He partially recovered, but never was able to do physical labor again. Because of his injuries, Crowell was forced to close the fluorspar mine temporarily, and the fate of Crowell, Jr., who was only a year away from graduation from Stanford University, was forever changed (J. I. and D. Crowell, 1987).

The younger Crowell was forced to withdraw from Stanford because of deteriorating family finances. After a short stint at the less expensive University of California at Los Angeles, he got a job in the booming southern California steel industry at U.S. Steel's plant in Torrance. Several years later, a comment by a fellow worker whom he respected caused him to alter the course of his life. The fellow worker told him he was "a plain damn fool" for working for others if he had a fluorspar mine. Crowell did some checking into the market for fluorspar in southern California, and after receiving assurances that U.S. Steel, and later Bethlehem Steel, would purchase his fluorspar, he returned to Beatty in 1927 to work the mine (J. I. and D. Crowell, 1987).

Upon his return to Beatty in 1927, Crowell, Jr., and Louis Vidano, who had faithfully remained in touch with the family, worked the fluorspar mine. The two men drilled and blasted by day and hoisted a few buckets of ore to the surface before going home at day's end. Crowell would return to town, eat, and then go back to the mine and work a second shift, climbing down the 134-foot shaft, loading a bucket with the purple ore, then climbing to the surface to hoist the ore and dump it. Then he would repeat the tedious, slow process. This he did until about 10 o'clock every night, seven days a week (J. I. and D. Crowell, 1987).

In 1928, Crowell married his Los Angeles sweetheart, Dorothy. Prior to the marriage, Dorothy made a trip to Beatty with Crowell's mother to see if she liked the town and would want to live there. She found it agreeable, and the newlyweds set up housekeeping in the home the family still owns. The small-town desert community was a big change for Dorothy Crowell. There were no conveniences. Their house had only one spigot of running water, no electricity, and "there was no indoor 'biffy,'" she remembered. Baths were taken in a wash-bowl in the kitchen; water was heated on the stove in the winter and in a sun-warmed tank in the summer. The one convenience available in Beatty in 1928 was the telegraph, a necessity for the T&T Railroad (J. I. and D. Crowell, 1987). The nearest emergency health care was in Las Vegas, then a small community and a full day's drive away over very poor dirt roads. All nonemergency medical care was obtained in Los Angeles (J. I. and D. Crowell, 1987).

Both J. Irving, Jr., and Dorothy had relatives in southern California, so they made regular trips to that area. Trips to Los Angeles were true expeditions compared to the 5-hour jour-ney in the 1990s. A trip from Beatty to Los Angeles by car took the Crowells three days. There were two possible routes: The first was north up Oasis Valley and across Sarcobatus Flat to the cutoff at Lida, over Westgard Pass and the White Moun-tains, and down into the Owens Valley. This leg of the journey, over dirt roads, took one day. They typically spent the first

night in Big Pine, California. The next day they again drove
over dirt roads as far as Mojave. At the end of the third day
they would arrive in Los Angeles. The alternate route took
them from Beatty to Las Vegas and on to Searchlight. From
Searchlight they would travel to Goffs (following the Santa Fe
tracks) and then west to Ludlow and Barstow, with dirt roads
all the way to the summit of Cajon Pass. The tire problems
encountered on these trips are nightmares by modern standards. In those days travelers did not carry spares; they
carried casings, tubes, and patching. A flat tire meant remov-
ing the tire and patching the tube, replacing the tube and
casing using clincher rims, and then pumping the tire up by
hand. On one trip to Los Angeles, the Crowells had 28 flats,
though several per day was a more usual figure. Trips to Las
Vegas became more frequent after the closure of the T&T
Railroad in 1940, because necessities were no longer shipped
by rail (J. I. and D. Crowell, 1987).

Except for sporadic shutdowns during some of the worst
years of the Depression in the 1930s, the Crowell fluorspar
mine operated almost continuously between 1927 and 1989,
producing in excess of 200,000 tons. It was a steady source of
employment for a handful of miners, and at times employment peaked at 15 to 20 men. The ore pinches in and out, and
the workings have varied over the years from only 6 inches to
70 or 80 feet in width. The small dump (where waste rock is
disposed of) belies the mine's longevity because the Crowells
have almost always dug on shipping-grade rock (J. I. and D.
Crowell, 1987; J. and M-K. Crowell, 1987).

In 1939, J. Irving Jr., acquired the first compressor for his
fluorspar mine from the old Gold Ace Mine located near
Carrara. It had two big flywheels and one cylinder, about 14
inches in diameter, and a glow plug that was heated with a
blowtorch to get it started. It ran on a low-grade diesel fuel. In

the early 1950s, Crowell installed a six-cylinder International Harvester to run his compressor (J. I. and D. Crowell, 1987; J. and M-K. Crowell, 1987).

For 30 years, Crowell used the same old Fairbanks-Morse single-cylinder gasoline engine for a hoist. In about 1951 he installed a 25-horsepower, three-phase electric hoist. The electricity was generated by a 125-horsepower International diesel with a 50-kw generator. The generator also supplied electric lights to the mine (J. and M-K. Crowell, 1987, 1989).

The abandonment of three railroads in the Beatty area meant that for years miners did not lack mine timbers in the treeless desert. Railroad ties were so abundant and so easily accessible that they filled the need. Because railroad ties are 8 feet long by 8 inches wide, many tunnels in the older part of the Crowell Mine are 8 feet high and 8 feet wide, roomy by the standard of small mine operations. Some of the old ties used in the Crowell Mine still have railroad spikes sticking in them. The Crowell Mine still has the original headframe that was put in the 1920s, although it has occasionally been strengthened (J. and M-K. Crowell, 1987).

The price of fluorspar has varied from about $11 a ton in 1917 to $23 a ton in the 1920, to $11 again in the Depression, and to the $60 range during the 1980s. Shipments averaged 500 to 600 tons of ore per month for many years. The fluorspar market has changed. At first fluorspar was sold to steel producers in southern California; more recently, with reductions in the amount of steel produced in the United States, the market has shifted to cement companies. In recent years, the ore was trucked from the Crowell Mine; in the early days, it was shipped on the railroad. After the closure of the T&T, the Crowells trucked the ore to Las Vegas, where it was put on the railroad. In recent years buyers provided their own transportation (J. I. and D. Crowell, 1987; J. and M-K. Crowell, 1987). The mine closed in 1989. If market conditions change, it might reopen.

The Crowells raised two sons in Beatty: Jack was born in 1931 and Don in 1934. Both children attended the Beatty schools in the lower grades and went to high school in Las Vegas. After graduating from the University of Nevada in 1953 with a degree in mining engineering, Jack worked briefly in Telluride, Colorado, and joined the Navy in 1954. He returned to Beatty in 1957 and joined his father in operating the fluorspar mine (J. and M-K. Crowell, 1987).

Jack Crowell was twelve years old when he started working three or four hours per day in his father's mine, helping the miners. The Crowell Mine then employed 12 people. Working with the rough-edged miners provided quite an education for the lad. Although given to some lurid descriptions and rough language, they were honest, hard-working people. Many were drifters and were on what miners still call "the circuit," a route that many miners travel, moving from one job to another. An idealized version of the route takes them from Arizona up to Idaho with the seasons—Arizona in the winter and Idaho in the summer. They never stay long on a job, perhaps only three to six months, and then they move on. But not all miners at the fluorspar mine were drifters on the circuit. Some were employed steadily by Crowell for ten or twelve years: Caesar Strozzi and his sons Joe and Harry, Ted "Bombo" Cottonwood, Gene Cross, and Harry Griffith (J. and M-K. Crowell, 1987).

Jack Crowell noted, with a bit of nostalgia, that mining has changed in recent years. A generation ago, mining was a profession, even an art. In the old days, he said, a miner had to know a little bit of everything: how to run and operate drilling equipment, how to blast, how to muck the ore and tram it and hoist it, how to hand-sort the waste rock from the valuable ore; he had to be a plumber, and he had to lay track. He needed the skills of a carpenter and a millwright for he had to timber a shaft, a drift, or a stope, and he had to build ore chutes. Today a miner is a specialist; he usually operates a specific type of equipment: The modern miner can run a dragline, a rubber-tired loader, or a 100-ton dump truck (J. and M-K. Crowell, 1987).

Early Milling Activity

Because of its railroads and the availability of water, Beatty was considered a convenient site for constructing mills to process ores mined in the region. In 1907 John W. Brock, the wealthy Philadelphian who owned the Tonopah Mining Company, purchased a major interest in the Tecopa Consolidated Mining Company and talked of building a $1.5 million smelter at Beatty. His plan was to use the lead ore from the Tecopa mine as a flux to treat the lower-grade, silicious ores from Tonopah and Goldfield. Tight money forced him to abandon his smelter idea and sell his shares in the company (Lingenfelter, 1986:357).

After the failure of the Bullfrog district, there were rumors that there was still high-grade to be found in the mines. Of particular interest was the Original Bullfrog Mine, with its famous high-grade, which legend said had once been displayed in the windows of Tiffany's. There were reports that the mine had produced $2 million (a wild exaggeration) and that a rich vein had faulted and been lost. In 1924, two leasers sank a shallow shaft at the mine and hit high-grade that ran $2600 a ton. They assumed they had found the lost "faulted vein," but shipped only a few thousand dollars' worth of ore. A number of people continued to work this property over the years, and one group even built a small mill at Beatty to process what they dug out (Lingenfelter, 1986:412).

Prior to the closure of the railroads, Beatty served as a railhead for many small mines in the area after the boom period was over. For example, leasers working lead claims after 1916 in the Ubehebe district on the northern slopes of the Panamint Range struck pockets of high-grade ore running about $100 a ton, and in 1921 and 1928, they shipped 1500 tons to the railhead at Beatty at a good profit (Lingenfelter, 1986:418–419).

In 1925, Charles Courtney Julian—a farmboy from the plains of Manitoba who became a flamboyant promoter involved in a multi-million-dollar oil swindle in California—formed the Western Lead Mines Company; he claimed he had found a fabulous deposit of lead at the head of Titus Canyon in the Grapevine Mountains. Buildings were constructed at the site, two tunnels were started, and a town called Leadfield was laid out. A road over the Grapevines to Beatty was constructed at a cost of between $40,000 and $60,000. Telephone and telegraph lines were run from Beatty (Lingenfelter, 1986:428–430). The company employed one hundred men. In January 1926, shares of Western Lead began selling on the Los Angeles Stock Exchange. The promotion reached a climax in March, when the "Julian Special" left Los Angeles with eleven Pullman sleepers, two diners, an observation car, and 340 enthusiasts on board. Eight hundred people drove down from Tonopah and Goldfield for the affair. On Sunday morning the enthusiasts made the 22-mile trek from Beatty to Leadfield over Julian's road. Stock jumped to a high of $3.30 on a 10-cent par. But the bubble soon burst; Julian's mine was exposed as a fraud, with his ore running less than $10 a ton and with only 200 tons in sight (Lingenfelter, 1986:430–431). Proving that a sucker *is* born every minute, Julian later returned to the people he had swindled on the Leadfield deal and bilked them again on a bogus silver mine in Arizona (Lingenfelter, 1986:433).

Conclusion

The town of Beatty was created by the excitement of the Bullfrog-Rhyolite boom, which was based on the hope that the gold deposits in the Bullfrog Hills were both rich and deep. They were neither. Rhyolite and all the other small communities it spawned faded almost as quickly as they began. Beatty, however, had something going for it—location. In their history of Rhyolite, Harold and Lucile Weight wrote, "Beatty . . . was on the natural, shortest, best-watered route between Goldfield and Las Vegas. Any main road, any railroad, was certain to go that way—as the highway goes today" (Weight, 1972:14). Beatty's accessibility and water supply made it possible for the small community to get through the first few years that are so critical in determining whether a Western boomtown will survive.

Once a nucleus at Beatty had proven that it could survive after 1910, it became the economic and social center for a very large geographical area.

CHAPTER 5

The Late 1920s to World War II

ike the desert flowers in the spring, the two-score or more of towns that formed in the wake of the heat and excitement of the Bullfrog boom seemed to appear almost overnight out of the rocky soil—only to disappear nearly as quickly. Each town's emergence was heralded as the beginning of something important, and at the time, it seemed as though all would last forever. Would not such names as Bullfrog, Gold Center, Pioneer, Leadfield, Chloride City, Carrara, Leeland, Lee, Rose's Well, Springdale, Bonnie Claire, Amargosa, Gold Crater, Johnnie, and others become permanent fixtures on the map of the American West—as solid and as enduring as the stone for which the area's mother camp, Rhyolite, was named? It was not to be. The veins of precious metal in the barren mountains that fed each town were as thin and unpredictable as the desert rains that watered the blossoms of spring. Like the flowers, the towns would not endure long. They would have their colorful moments in the sun, and then they would disappear into the rocky desert soil from which they sprang.

There was one exception: Beatty. As the other towns faded, it hung on. Situated about half-way between Las Vegas and Tonopah on the main north-south roadway in Nevada, and with plenty of readily accessible water, Beatty, though it remained small, became the economic nucleus for a vast area that encompassed more than 50 miles in any direction in southern Nevada and the eastern California desert region.

Economic activity in Beatty in the late 1920s and early 1930s included some mining, an assortment of local merchants, the distribution of oil and gas, the construction of Death Valley Scotty's Castle during the late 1920s, and the production and sale of illegal alcohol during Prohibition.

Mining Slacks Off

There were only a few mines in operation in the area—at Pioneer and Rhyolite—during the early part of this period: Rube Bryan owned the Mayflower Mine in Pioneer; Louis McCrea, a member of a prominent Beatty family, came to the area in the Rhyolite days and worked his mine at Chloride Cliff for years; and J. I. Crowell, Jr., operated his fluorspar mine on Bare Mountain (J. and M-K. Crowell, 1987; A. Revert, 1987; R. and C. Lisle, 1987).

But sometimes people who were not even miners often stumbled on ways to make a profit from a mine. Tailor Bill Elliot's connection to the profits of the Gold Ace Mine is one of the most unusual Beatty tales.

The Gold Ace Mine, located on the west side of Bare Mountain, not far from Carrara and several miles south of Beatty, was discovered in the early years of the Bullfrog boom. At times, the mine produced some very rich gold ore, but production was often "on and off" because to the "pockety" character of the ore's occurrence. In March 1929, Roland Wiley, a young lawyer who was living in Las Vegas and later went on to become district attorney for Clark County, rode from Las Vegas to Reno with Bill Elliot, who had owned a tailor shop in Los Angeles. Elliot had operated tailor shops in Tonopah and Goldfield during those town's boom days and had intended to open another shop in Reno. Elliot was very well known for his craftsmanship and had won a national award for a coat he made.

On their way to Reno, Wiley and Elliot stopped at Carrara where they learned from Briz Putnam and Jim Shay, two former Tonopah and Goldfield miners who were in charge of the Gold Ace Mine, that things were not going well. No good ore was in sight and Gold Ace stock was worth only 3 cents per share. Not long after Elliot opened his Reno shop, Harry Stimler, co-discoverer of the rich strike that resulted in the Goldfield boom in 1902, talked Elliot into trading him two tailor-made suits for 5000 shares of Gold Ace stock. Elliot agreed; at the stockmarket price he would receive the equivalent of about $75 each for the suits, a fair price for a tailor-made suit at that time.

Late that spring, however, fortune changed at the Gold Ace when a pocket of very rich gold ore was found. There was considerable excitement associated with the discovery of the rich ore, and a man named Bixby, a member of a prominent Long Beach, California, family who had invested in the mine, chartered a promotional train from Los Angeles to Beatty to publicize the good luck and to help move the stock's price up. Roland Wiley came up from Las Vegas to Carrara to participate in the festivities, which were timed to coincide with the July 4 celebration. A big tent had been set up, plenty of alcoholic beverages were available, and samples of the ore, in which free milling gold could clearly be seen, were on display. As a result of the discovery of the ore the price of the Gold Ace stock temporarily shot up. That summer Elliot sold the 5000 shares of Gold Ace stock he had obtained from Stimler for more than $1 a share, thus making Stimler's suits the most expensive in the state of Nevada (Wiley, 1991).

By the late 1930s, mining activity in Beatty had increased somewhat in comparison to the level of a few years earlier. The Roosevelt administration had raised the price of gold, which stimulated a number of small operations in central Nevada. As the only community of consequence in a vast area, Beatty was a natural trade center for the miners. Ralph Lisle remembered the mining activity at Skidoo and Pioneer, with 20 or 30 men working at Bullfrog and a few less at Rhyolite. There was also activity at other area mines—the Keane Wonder, the Chloride Cliff, the Ubehebe, the Gold Ace, the Panama on Bare Mountain, and the Diamond Queen; in 1940 the payroll at Carrara frequently reached 200 (R. and C. Lisle, 1987; "Beatty Shows Population Growth in Past Decade," 1950).

The Reverts Boost the Beatty Economy

The Revert family was typical of many that came to Nevada and made contributions to the economy. Albert Revert, patriarch of the Revert family of Beatty, was born in Le Havre, France, September 20, 1869; when he was a small child, he immigrated to the United States with his family. The Reverts first lived in New York City, but when Albert's mother died, he and his father made their way to San Francisco and later to Virginia City, where young Albert attended the Fourth Ward School. At age eleven he found a job working in a box factory in nearby Verdi, and he lived with a French family there (A. Revert, 1987).

In Verdi, young Albert worked hard and prospered. But even as a child, he did not like working for other people. He worked in sawmills and also began to buy fresh fish from the Indians in the Reno area for shipment on ice to the Palace

Hotel in San Francisco. He acted as an interpreter for the French Canadians in the Verdi area (A. Revert, 1987; R. Revert, 1988).

Albert moved to Tonopah shortly after the great silver boom began in 1900. By this time, Revert had mastered every aspect of the lumber business, and he established a lumber yard on the north side of town at the site of the old Conley Yard. His Tonopah Lumber Company (which owned a large number of horses, mules, and wagons) hauled lumber from Mina to Tonopah prior to construction of the railroad. It was one of several firms that transported supplies. In all, 400 horses in teams of 12 to 20 were involved (Myrick, 1962:237).

Revert married Henrietta Bucking, a San Francisco woman whose parents had come from Germany. Their first child, Art, was born in San Francisco in late 1905 and shortly thereafter—not long after the great San Francisco earthquake—mother and baby joined Albert in Tonopah. The family resided in Tonopah for several years, until Art and his mother moved back to the San Francisco area. Art completed high school in Oakland, California. Meanwhile, the family had grown to include three additional children, Edith, Norman, and Robert (A. Revert, 1987; R. Revert, 1988).

Albert eventually became the owner of a large sawmill in Verdi and a string of lumber yards in virtually every community of consequence in Nevada, including Fallon, Sparks, Elko, and Reno. With profits from his Tonopah Lumber Company, Revert purchased the Verdi Lumber Company in 1908 from Oliver Lonkey. Originally there were several partners in the Verdi firm, including Jack Salisbury; but by the late 1920s, Revert was sole owner. In addition to wood products, he sold hardware, wagons, and automobiles. He owned no lumber yards in the southern part of the state because there was little business activity there at that time. These widely dispersed business holdings were blessed with honest and competent help who did not require constant supervision or oversight (A. Revert, 1987; R. Revert, 1988; Myrick, 1962: 411).

After completing high school, Art joined his father in the lumber business in Verdi, working at general duties, including grading lumber. Times were good for the company. There was considerable business in the production of doors and sashes and molding for decorative trim. The pine wood from the region was especially suited to such uses because it did not crack or split when a nail was driven through it. One of the biggest markets was New York. Often, several railroad cars loaded with the company's products were in transit, necessitating large amounts of credit. Things went well until a few years before the Depression (A. Revert, 1987).

A number of serious fires proved to be the company's undoing. There was one during World War I, which was believed to have been set by a German agent. Another fire in the 1920s was caused by a whirlwind that scattered hot coals over the mill area. The most serious fire (in 1926) burned the entire Verdi sawmill. Robert Revert remembered the 1926 fire and recalled that the hill behind Verdi was red with flame. (Only in recent years have the trees begun to grow back.) Revert had recently cut all the timber he was planning to mill that season, and he asked the Forest Service to let him out of his contract because of the fire, but his request was refused. A modest mill was assembled, but it was not enough; the company went bankrupt, in part because of inadequate insurance (R. Revert, 1988).

After the Reverts' lumber business was wiped out, the family looked around the state for, as Art said, "a place to land." Albert and son Art arrived in Beatty on New Year's Eve, 1929. They chose Beatty because a mine at Chloride Cliff looked promising. Albert had purchased a Chloride Cliff property (not the same property that J. Irving Crowell, Jr., had worked) in partnership with three men—W. R. McRae, a man from Reno who was the owner of the Overland Hotel, and an ex-governor of Idaho. The unexpected deaths of two of the three investors led to the failure of the enterprise (A. Revert, 1987).

Revert then decided to purchase the Shirk estate from Shirk's daughter, for approximately $10,000. The estate included the old Beatty Ranch, consisting of 300 acres, the stone cabin once occupied by Old Man Beatty, and considerable water rights; a primitive community water system that obtained water from the Beatty Ranch and supplied it to a small number of town residents; a number of pieces of property in town; and a store, known as the Amargosa Land and Cattle Company (sometimes called Palmer's Store, after a former owner), housed in a large, iron-clad building at the north end of town (A. Revert, 1987; R. Revert, 1988).

The store, renamed the Revert Mercantile, was the largest in town. It carried anything a person in an isolated desert community could possibly need: a variety of canned goods; fresh meat that was shipped in by rail from Ottumwa, Iowa; mining supplies, including picks, shovels, drilling steel, and dynamite and caps (that were stored in a powder house on the hill east of town). Revert did big business in the sale of coal, which was brought in on the railroad by the carload and sold by the sack.

The Reverts had acquired the Union Oil distributorship shortly after they arrived. They built a Union Oil service station in town and soon had gas pumps in Rhyolite, Gold Point, Ash Meadows, Hot Springs, and Springdale; these locations required only a tank and a visible pump, which sold for $35 or $40. At Rhyolite an old caboose and pump served as the service station. The Revert trucks made deliveries to the pumps, and the local owners bought the gas at wholesale prices. There were three problems with being in the petroleum business in Beatty, Art Revert recalled: bad roads, long distance, and the difficulty of collecting money (A. Revert, 1987).

One of the first things the Reverts did after their purchase in 1930 was to upgrade and improve the primitive water system that was part of the Shirk estate. They patched pipe and extended distribution to additional families in town. The charge for water service was $4 a month per customer (A. Revert, 1987).

Some years later State Health Department officials analyzed water being supplied to Beatty. Their analysis revealed excessively high levels of fluoride in the water obtained from the spring on the Beatty Ranch. (The water stained the teeth of children; Art Revert remembered that the teeth of the Indian children were especially stained.) State officials found the water quality unacceptable, and the Reverts turned their operation over to the Beatty Water Company, which was owned by a general improvement district. The company dug a well on the edge of the ballpark between Third and Fourth Streets and piped in additional water from wells drilled in the hills to the west of Beatty; this source diluted the fluoride in the water from the ballpark well. Water from those wells became the source of community water (A. Revert, 1987).

In May 1953, Albert Revert, who in his later years became known as "Dad," passed away at the age of 83. His obituary in the *Beatty Bulletin* described his birth in France, his residence in Virginia City, and the eventual establishment of the lumber company in Verdi. It described how Revert had first arrived in Tonopah, his skill in handling 22-mule teams over rough trails, and in making complicated driving maneuvers. "Always a great booster for his community," the article stated, "and the State of Nevada, Mr. Revert had a wealth of friends who looked forward to visiting him at every opportunity. His ready wit and keen mind never deserted him, and he maintained his interest in national and world affairs to the end" ("Beatty Mourns Passing of Beloved Dad Revert," 1953).

Robert Revert described his father as a self-educated man with a keen insight, an observant individual with a fast mind, and a man who did everything for his family. He also added that Henrietta Revert, who was fluent in three languages— English, French, and German—had an "even disposition and was a good cook, seamstress, bookkeeper, and was a wonderful mother" (R. Revert, 1988).

Other Economic Activity

In addition to Revert Mercantile, there were two other stores in town: one owned by the Richings family (operated by "Mom" Richings) and the other by Cy Johnson. H. H. ("Pop") Richings operated the Standard Oil dealership. Beatty had its share of bars, including the Gold Ace, St. Peters' Bar (run by Glen St. Peters), and the Exchange Club (originally built and still being run at that time by George Greenwood). The Gold Ace burned down about 1940—many residents remembered the fire. Joe Andre's Silver Diner and a fountain in the Exchange Club were popular restaurants (R. and C. Lisle, 1987; A. Revert, 1987; C. Lisle, 1989).

The T&T Railroad employed several townspeople in Beatty. Before the roads in and out of town were paved, nearly all goods came into town from the south on the railroad. Dave Aspen was then the railroad agent; he had originally worked in Tonopah for the railroad (A. Revert, 1987).

Lisle Contributes to Beatty's Transportation Economy

The widespread availability of the automobile added a new dimension to transportation and economic activity in southcentral Nevada. Though the automobile clearly had its advantages in the area, the conveniently scheduled railroad service at first provided stiff competition to the horseless carriage as the mode of travel between the region's widely separated towns. However, as railroad schedules were first reduced and then eventually eliminated entirely, the automobile came into its own. It emerged as the transportation means of choice (the only other alternatives were foot, horse or burro, and wagon).

The growing popularity of the automobile created new economic opportunities in Beatty as well as other communities. Service stations—as they were properly termed in those days—were opened to meet motorists' needs for gas, tires, repairs, directions, and a friendly word. Service stations gradually became an important factor in Beatty's economy and continue to contribute significantly to the area.

The automobile and the service stations it spawned represented a change in the way people lived and the way they thought about life and the world, but not everyone saw the advantages, including some of the old "jackass" prospectors. In his book *50 Years in Death Valley—Memoirs of a Borax Man,* Harry P. Gower tells of a chance meeting he and William W. Cahill (both officials with the Pacific Coast Borax Company, which owned the T&T) had with an old-timer who was having difficulties with his preferred means of transportation. The old-timer exhibited an intuitive grasp of the close link between transportation mode and lifestyle:

> I might as well tell of the time [W. W.] Cahill and I were driving along in a Model A Ford towards Goldfield 40 miles away. We stopped to chat with an old prospector who was having some trouble packing up his burros. He had been heading towards Goldfield too, but his animals had broken

loose and only just been rounded up after a three-day chase. Cahill said, "Shucks, why don't you get rid of those damn troublemakers? Get a Ford and you would be in Goldfield in two hours." After thinking that over the old man said, "I guess you're right but what would I do when I get there?" (Gower, 1969:138).

The old prospector knew getting there was most of the fun. Nonetheless, the automobile was clearly here to stay and many, including Ralph Lisle, saw economic opportunity in its arrival. Ralph Lisle, the son of John Quincy and Celesta Fairbanks Lisle, was the grandson of Ralph J. "Dad" Fairbanks, a southern Nevada–Mojave Desert pioneer and town builder. Lisle was born in Fernley, Nevada, in 1914, but spent most of his life in the Beatty–Death Valley area (R. and C. Lisle, 1987).

Lisle has vivid memories of the move his family made in 1926 from their family homestead in Fernley, just east of Reno, to Clay Camp in Ash Meadows in the Amargosa Valley. They caravanned in a Model-T pickup and a Dodge touring car on dirt roads for three days. On the first leg of the journey, they drove from Fernley to Yerington and then on to Schurz, where they spent the night. The next day they drove to Goldfield. (Because the highway followed the railroad tracks, they bypassed Tonopah on their way to Goldfield.) They spent the night at the Goldfield Hotel, which was a treat to the impressionable young Lisle. The next day they drove through Beatty to Clay Camp (R. and C. Lisle, 1987).

After Ralph Lisle graduated from high school, he worked for two years for his grandfather, "Dad" Fairbanks in Baker, California, and for seven years for his uncle, Charlie Brown, in Shoshone, California. Working for Fairbanks and Brown amounted to a quality apprenticeship in the management and operation of gas stations and general stores in the Death

Valley region. In 1938, Brown sent Lisle to Beatty to reactivate the Standard Oil distributorship, which had closed down early in the Depression, and the service station that they had recently purchased form H. H. Richings. (The other distributorship—Union Oil—was owned by the Reverts.)

Lisle and his wife, Chloe (whom he had married in 1939), operated the station until the outbreak of World War II, when both the distributorship and station were deemed a nonessential industry and were forced to close. Lisle switched to the mining of minerals, which was considered essential for the war effort. Later he entered military service. After the war, he returned home and found that the ownership of the Standard Oil distributorship had been transferred in his absence. Later, the Lisles opened a Union 76 station on Second Street across from the Exchange Club.

The Bootleg Business

Perhaps the most important business in the Beatty area during Prohibition was illegal: the production and distribution of homemade booze. In fact, the bootleg business was so active in Beatty that, as one old-timer said, "You could smell the town coming." Many residents made their own beer.

The Beatty area bootleggers used sugar rather than grain in their manufacturing process, and much of the sugar was purchased at the Revert Mercantile. Distilleries were fired with kerosene, again purchased locally. Both the sugar and kerosene came into town on the T&T Railroad. There was "spirited competition" among the area's producers concerning who made the best whiskey; but even the best produced then, old-timers say, was not good whiskey by today's standards. The product was sold in bottles, jugs, barrels—anything that would hold liquid. It was sold as far away as Ely and California. Some was sold in Death Valley (A. Revert, 1987).

Law enforcers were a constant problem for the bootleggers, but some authorities were known to look the other way. Local producers were usually tipped off if federal officials were heading for Beatty. Word would come in over the telegraph: "The blackbirds are flying today." It was deemed necessary to provide law enforcement officials with token arrests, so producers and sellers took turns at getting "knocked off." Those arrested would go before the court and be fined, but would quickly be back in business. A minor era in Beatty's history ended when Prohibition was repealed in 1933 (A. Revert, 1987).

Scotty's Castle: "Neither of Us Pays Rent"

Construction of Scotty's Castle, which began in 1925, had a notable effect on Beatty, the closest town to the site. Walter Edward Scott, better known as Death Valley Scotty, was born in Cyanthiana, Kentucky, on September 20, 1872, and came to Nevada at the age of fourteen; he became skilled as a cowhand and at bronco busting. After a stint with Buffalo Bill Cody's Wild West Show, he ended up in the Death Valley area where he put his greatest talents to use—as a quintessential flimflam man. Richard Lingenfelter described Scotty as "a ham actor, a conscienceless con man, an almost pathological liar, and a charismatic bullslinger" (1986:242). Scotty would do almost anything for attention and publicity and could pry a dollar out of the most tight-fisted businessman. Scotty's Castle—probably his greatest con—involved Albert M. Johnson, a wealthy capitalist from Chicago. Johnson, the son of an Oberlin, Ohio, banker, had graduated from Cornell University in 1895. He began amassing his own wealth by speculating in the Missouri zinc mining boom with money borrowed from his father. He eventually acquired control of the National Life Insurance Company in 1902 (Lingenfelter, 1986:256).

An article in the *Beatty Bulletin* gave Scotty's version of how he persuaded Johnson to underwrite the construction of a great mansion at the mouth of Grapevine Canyon at the north end of Death Valley.

> I always wanted a castle in Death Valley, so one time, several years ago, when I was in Chicago I thought I'd see about getting it. I noticed a huge skyscraper and asked a policeman who owned it.
>
> "That belongs to a big insurance company," he said. I asked him who the head man was, and he replied, "The president, of course, A. M. Johnson."
>
> So I got in the elevator and rode to the top floor where I asked for Mr. Johnson. He was very cordial, and inquired, "What can I do for you, young man?"
>
> "I live in the desert and want to build a Castle," I told him. "I figure it should cost about a million and a half dollars. I thought maybe you'd give it to me."
>
> "Why, of course," Johnson said, going to his safe. Then he stopped and remarked, "I'm not sure a million and a half is enough. Better take two million."
>
> "So I took the two million and came out here and built the Castle," Scotty concluded straight-faced ("District Loses True Friend in Death of A. M. Johnson," 1948).

The castle, called "one of the wonders of the world," was featured in the *Saturday Evening Post*, and for 18 days stories about it appeared on the front page of the *Los Angeles Record*. The castle became so famous that it even upstaged Scotty, who refused to sleep in his $40,000 bedroom in the castle, prefer-ring a small bungalow several miles down the canyon, or if the

Johnsons were not there, sleeping on a cot amid dirty dishes and pans in the kitchen (Lingenfelter, 1986:461–463). The mansion, located in the middle of nowhere, had its own water supply, sewer system, hydroelectric generator, cold storage, ice plant, air conditioning, and solar heating. Interior work was accomplished by European artisans and craftsmen. Johnson furnished the building with custom and antique items obtained from extended buying trips. When it was completed, the castle boosted Beatty's economy by becoming a major tourist attraction (Lingenfelter, 1986:448, 462).

As Lingenfelter (1986:461) has pointed out, Death Valley Scotty was the personification of Death Valley for many years, a major attraction in himself, as fascinating as the mountains and the valley whose name he bore as a nickname. Scotty had always had a flair for cultivating publicity. Though Johnson put up the estimated $2.5 million for the castle, Johnson was more than content to let Scotty give the world the impression that it was Scotty's, constructed with Scotty's millions.

> ... the story is told of the persistent tourist who wanted to know definitely who owned the Castle, Johnson or Scotty. Ever a master of evasion, Mr. Johnson replied:
> "Well, my friend, it's like this. Scotty lives here and I live here, and neither of us pays rent" ("District Loses True Friend in Death of A. M. Johnson," 1948).

In January 1948, when Johnson died, the *Beatty Bulletin* reported, "In Mr. Johnson's death, the West, and particularly this district has lost a loyal friend." The story continued.

> Scotty did not attend Mr. Johnson's funeral fearing that he might break down under the strain, for the desert philosopher is a man of advanced years himself, and will mark his

76th birthday on September 20. Scotty was present at funeral services for Mrs. Johnson several years ago, and was so moved that he reportedly told his partner at the time that he would never go through a similar ordeal.

"I prefer to remember Johnson as he was in life," Scotty said simply ("District Loses True Friend in Death of A. M. Johnson," 1948).

Johnson's body had been in the ground scarcely more than four months when a new facet was added to the incredible tale. The *Beatty Bulletin* ran the following article.

SECRET GOLD HOARD HIDDEN AT CASTLE?

NO TRACE FOUND OF RICH CACHE OWNED BY JOHNSON

What Happened to 7500-oz Gold Dust Treasure Trove After Johnson Died?

A secret cache of over 7500 oz. of gold dust valued at about a quarter of a million dollars, remains unaccounted for in the will and behests of A. M. Johnson, wealthy Los Angeles philanthropist and religious zealot, who died last January. . . . The possible existence of the modern "pot of gold" was disclosed by Walter Scott (Death Valley Scotty) and confirmed by executive personnel of Scotty's Castle, some 60 miles from Beatty and Goldfield, who said that they knew of the treasure trove before Johnson's death but had no inkling as to its present whereabouts.

Scotty avowed that two years ago Johnson made a trip to his ranch, located a short distance from the Castle, and produced several bags of almost pure gold dust which he had accumulated through the years. Where it came from

Scotty could not say, and Johnson was reluctant about telling him.

The two men secretly weighed the precious material, finding that it totalled slightly over 7533 oz., according to Scotty. Later, Johnson mentioned the matter to Mr. and Mrs. Henry Ringe, who managed the castle, and indicated that he was puzzled as to how he would ultimately dispose of the gold.

Johnson, a meticulous man, had carefully provided for the disposition of virtually every article of his worldly goods before his death, but nowhere was there any mention made of the quarter of a million dollars worth of gold dust, Scotty said.

Since Johnson had customarily taken him into his confidence on matters of importance, Scotty is puzzled to know what became of the treasure, and indicated that he had conducted private searches in the Castle and around the grounds without unearthing any clues. He appears to believe that Johnson secreted the gold somewhere in the neighborhood, "but died sooner than he expected."

Sometime last summer, while low in spirits, Johnson again mentioned the rich hoard to Scotty, and seemed as perplexed as ever as to what he should do with it. He vaguely made mention of taking it to Mexico, Scotty said, but whether he ever did or not Scotty could not say ("Secret Gold Hoard Hidden at Castle?" 1948).

The alleged cache of gold would have weighed more than 627 pounds, no easy task for an old man to stash alone. At 1991 gold prices, it would be worth more than $2.75 million.

Six years after Johnson died, in January 1954, Walter Edward (Death Valley Scotty) Scott, died. In the obituary in the *Beatty Bulletin*, Scotty was described as one of the last remaining links with the early West: "Death overtook him on Nevada soil, where in his younger days he wrote so many colorful chapters in the state's history." Scotty is buried on a hill near the castle that bears his name ("Scotty Buried on Hill Near Famed Castle," 1954).

People of Beatty

The people who called Beatty home came from many places, led a variety of lifestyles, and brought to the community their unique personalities and talents. All left their mark on Beatty.

Swiss-born Caesar Strozzi was struck with "gold fever" and migrated to the United States; for a time he worked in Rhyolite. His wife, Mary, was a full-blooded Western Shoshone and a member of the Te'moak Band, which lived in the Elko area. The couple and their seven children did not reside within the Indian community on the east side of town, but lived in the south part of Beatty (Gillette, 1987, 1989).

In the 1920s Strozzi homesteaded at Briar Spring, northwest of Beatty, in the Grapevine Mountains. He constructed a home and several outbuildings—five buildings in all in addition to dugouts (Latschar, 1981:230). The Strozzis, who spent about half of the year at Briar Spring, would usually leave for the ranch in early May and seldom returned to Beatty before the latter part of October. Strozzi cultivated a variety of crops on the ranch, primarily for his family's consumption. Irrigation was needed to produce corn and vegetables as well as apples, pears, and peaches. Strozzi also raised some chickens and cattle. The cattle were usually rounded up in the winter and moved down from the high country because of the cold weather. The ranch was occupied by Strozzi until the late 1940s. Caesar Strozzi died in 1953 and his wife, Mary, passed away in 1963. Dolly Gillette, one of the Strozzi children, still resides in Beatty (Gillette, 1987).

Grace Whitten Davies arrived in Beatty in 1937 and married Fred Davies, who had previously lived in Ash Meadows and had moved to Beatty a few years earlier (Davies, 1987). Fred worked as a blacksmith and Grace was a waitress.

Joe Andre, a musician who had a dance band, played in Beatty and other small towns throughout Nevada during the 1930s. He pulled his well-constructed travel trailer with aluminum siding to the dance sites. When the dance band folded, Andre set the trailer up on a lot diagonally across from the Exchange Club in Beatty and operated a cafe called the Silver Diner. In the 1940s Andre acquired the Exchange Club from the Greenwood Estate and ran it for several years before turning it over to his son-in-law, Louis Hinds, who managed it for several years before Andre sold it to Warren Doing (R. Lisle, 1991).

During the 1920s and 1930s Beatty was home to an assortment of elderly, retired miners who had come to the district with the Bullfrog boom and had stayed on. Many were former members of the International Workers of the World (Wobblies) labor union, and though their names are now forgotten, they are best remembered for their outspoken leftist political beliefs.

According to the U.S. Census for 1940, Beatty was still quite small. The population of the township, which included those who lived in the area from Springdale, located at the head of Oasis Valley, to Lathrop Wells, now known as Amargosa Valley, was 450; most lived in Beatty ("Beatty Shows Population Growth in Past Decade," 1950). Ralph Lisle remembered there was no housing—not even a trail—west of Montgomery Street, "just sagebrush and rocks." Quite a number of houses had been moved in from Rhyolite and

Pioneer. Big cottonwood trees lined the wooden sidewalks of Main Street, and the fronts of many buildings had canopies. The trees, the canopies, and the wooden sidewalks were removed during the 1950s when the State Highway Department paved the road through Beatty and widened it in the process (A. Revert, 1987; J. and M-K. Crowell, 1987).

Electric Power and Waste Disposal

Until about 1940, Beatty had no electricity. The first supplier, Jim Mardis, obtained a franchise and provided a few families with electricity (C. Lisle, 1989). This system frequently broke down, never ran on a regular schedule, and could not be depended upon for refrigeration. About 1940, the Reverts obtained a government loan, bought out Mardis, and expanded the system. The new supplier, known as the Amargosa Power Company, bought four big International diesel engines equipped with 50-kilowatt generators, scrounged the desert for poles, and wired the town (Sternberg, 1986). Anybody who wanted electricity could sign up. The availability of electricity in Beatty allowed many people to purchase refrigerators. In 1950, street lights were installed in Beatty, first on Main Street and then on some of the side streets. Prior to that the only light after dark was from shops and stores open after sundown (A. Revert, 1987).

The four new engines were more than enough to handle the town's requirements. The system could get by much of the time on one engine and a heavy load required two. Occasionally a third engine was required, but four were never needed, leaving a reserve in case one failed. The extra engines did not kick in automatically upon increased demand, but had to be engaged manually. Art Revert had gauges installed in his house and could determine the need at a glance. The system ran 24 hours a day and required little maintenance—only twice-daily checks and periodic oil changes.

The Amargosa Power Company operated until April 1963 when the Nevada Public Service Commission approved its sale to the Valley Electric Association, an electric cooperative serving Pahrump and Amargosa valleys; the power was generated at Hoover Dam. Service with Valley Electric began with 194 customers in Beatty and 6 in Rhyolite (Sternberg, 1986; A. Revert, 1987; Records, 1987).

There was no community sewer system in Beatty as of 1949; nearly everyone had a septic system. Eventually there were so many septic systems that the groundwater was becoming contaminated. In the 1970s, a sanitation district was formed to put in a community-wide sewer system.

Phone Service

Communication with the rest of the world was late in coming to Beatty. A telegraph line served the town while the T&T was operating, but when the railroad shut down the line was removed. Fairly early during World War II, phone lines were strung from Las Vegas. Crowells' fluorspar mine, deemed an essential industry by the federal government, helped Beatty get a high priority, AA-1 rating, for the installation of phones. There was a switchboard in town and the operator was in Tonopah (J. I. and D. Crowell, 1987).

Eavesdroppers on the party line were sources of amusement. Before they were married, Maud-Kathrin Crowell recalled talking to Jack on the phone from her home in Boulder City. She heard a chiming clock strike the hour. "Your clock is fast, Jack," she said. "I just heard it strike the hour. It isn't 8:00 yet."

"We don't have a chiming clock," Jack replied.

They both heard a click on the party line (J. and M-K. Crowell, 1987).

But even in the late 1940s, it was still quite difficult to reach people in Beatty by phone. There were only two phones: a public phone in Brownie's Store, which was closed in the evening, and another in front of Azbill's Store (formerly the Revert Mercantile), where street noise and the phone's distance from homes made it difficult to use. A campaign was begun for installation of a public phone that would be "readily available at all times for both incoming and outgoing calls" ("Continue Efforts to Secure 'Night' Phone for Beatty," 1948). By the late 1950s, there were approximately 30 phones in Beatty (J. and M-K. Crowell, 1987). In about 1960 a modern dial phone system was installed (C. Lisle, 1989).

Pioneer Educators

In 1937, Ert Moore, a young school teacher, came to Beatty looking for a new job. His first position in Nevada, which he had held for two years, was at Deerlodge, an isolated area about 30 miles east of Pioche in Lincoln County (Moore, 1979:1–9). In 1937, when the enrollment fell to two students, Lincoln County closed the school. Hearing that teachers were needed in Goldfield and Beatty, he and his wife set out for Ely, then Tonopah, "over unpaved roads across sandy stretches when the car running boards would drag on the sides of the ruts" (Moore, 1979:17). They arrived in Goldfield only to find that the last vacancy had been filled. They hastened on to Beatty and found there was a vacancy. Moore met with the members of the school board—George Greenwood, who owned the Exchange Club along with an attached garage and grocery store that also included the post office; Tom Harris, who operated the Associated Gas Station and Garage located on Fourth and Main; and Bill McClosky, a miner from Idaho who had come to the Beatty area during the Rhyolite boom and operated a mining property at Chloride Cliff during the 1930s (R. Lisle, 1991).

A contract was drawn up; Moore's salary was to be $160 a month, a substantial increase over the $900 a year he had received in Lincoln County. Moore taught in Beatty for five years before moving to Gabbs in 1942 (Moore, 1979:17, 38, 40; C. Lisle, 1989). While he was employed in Beatty, Moore and his wife lived in a three-room miner's house that had been moved there from an abandoned mining camp, possibly Rhyolite.

Moore, who spent more 25 years as a teacher and educator in Nevada, described the Beatty school:

> The elementary school consisted of two rooms and toilets, and four grades were taught in each of the two rooms. This building was old but very sturdily constructed. The high school building consisted of a one-room structure brought in from some old mining camp. The dimensions of the building were about 12' x 20' and there was only one door. Heat came from an oil stove near the door, and the stove was between the students and the exit. . . . Playground equipment consisted of one backstop and goal for basketball for the older students and nothing for the younger ones to play with (Moore, 1979:19).

Old maps hung on the walls; when extra desks were needed, they could be obtained from Goldfield for $2 each (Moore, 1979:28). There were 10 students in the high school; 2 were Anglos and the rest were Indians. Of the 40 students in the elementary school, about 25 were Indians (Moore, 1979:20).

One Beatty resident remembered her first day at school after moving to Beatty from Los Angeles. Finding only about 3 children in her class, she was struck by how small it was in comparison to the schools she had attended in Los Angeles. "Is this all the kids?" she recalled asking her teacher.

The teacher replied, "Oh, no. Wait until the Indian kids come." They were out of town harvesting pine nuts.

In 1938, Fred Dees was hired to teach the upper grades. Dees was a mature and experienced teacher, and even today his former students speak fondly of him and credit success in college to the excellent education they received in his classes (J. and M-K. Crowell, 1987).

Moore described how he and Dees secured materials to construct some much-needed playground equipment for the younger children:

> We needed playground equipment first and no money was available. The old poles from a defunct telegraph line to Goldfield were still in place. Local information was that Death Valley Scotty owned them. I left word at the saloons that when Scotty came to town to tell him to drop by the school. One day he came chugging up in the old car that is on display at Scotty's Castle in Death Valley. I asked for enough poles to make playground equipment, which he so generously granted. He invited me to bring the family and visit him at the castle, which we did. Mr. Dees and I went to the pole line, secured our poles and made the necessary playground equipment, which was greatly enjoyed by the children.
>
> In the meantime, some county officials from Tonopah had heard of our school project. They came to the school and demanded to know why we took the old poles. When I told them that Scotty gave them to me they became furious and said that he was a damn liar, that he never owned them, and that they belonged to the County. They fumed around for awhile but told us to take no more. The equipment was used

by the children for over twenty-five years, and we were richly rewarded for our efforts, as the poles had been standing unused in the desert for over a quarter of a century. Death Valley Scotty had made a great contribution to the Beatty children.... This episode with Scotty was quite a joke among the town folk and around the saloons for a long time. The admiration of Scotty for his gift to the school was long lasting (Moore, 1979:23–24).

Moore and Dees also laid out a basketball court and installed a hoop; all the children enjoyed the game—especially the Indians, who were good athletes (Moore, 1979:21).

Children at Play

Though the town of Beatty was small and lacked recreational facilities, the children never wanted for things to do. At school during recess the younger children used the facilities Moore and Dees had constructed; the older ones played basketball or baseball on a field that was nothing more than a patch of desert strewn with rocks and brush. May Day, the first day of May, was an important occasion at the Beatty school. Instruction was suspended and the day was devoted to a variety of athletic activities, including foot races, long-jump and high-jump contests, and ball games. The Indian children often dominated; sometimes, the Indian girls outperformed the Anglo boys.

Boys derived great pleasure from playing marbles. A circle about 3 feet in diameter was scratched in the dirt and each player placed several marbles in the circle. The object of the game was to try to knock out the marbles that were inside the circle by "shooting" another marble from the outside. Holding a marble between thumb and index finger, the player used a flecking motion with the thumb to propel the "shooter" marble. The shooter marble, also known as a Tau, was a lad's most valuable marble. Players got to keep the marbles they knocked out of the circle. The families of Anglo boys in the community could often afford to buy their sons more marbles, which eventually ended up in possession of the poorer Indians, who were usually better players.

Another favorite activity of children in town was to roll their favorite old automobile tires. Children who had bikes often rode them to the hot springs located 5 miles north, though there was no pool there—the hot water emerged from a tunnel. Miners in town who lacked hot water in their cabins often used the springs for a Saturday night bath. Jack Crowell and a friend used to walk along the curb of Main Street of Beatty looking for discarded Bull Durham tobacco sacks, which they took home and filled with purple-colored fluorspar ore from the Crowell Mine for use in playing mining (J. Crowell, 1991). Girls played jacks and both girls and boys played a game called Red Rover. They would join hands and form two lines opposite each other; representatives from each line would alternately try to break through the other line. Games of hide-and-seek and kick-the-can were played by young people of Beatty even into their teens (J. Crowell, 1991). Sometimes a boy and girl who had hidden together might use the short time before their discovery to snuggle a bit.

For a time a movie was offered once a week in the old Town Hall. It was also considered great fun to go down to the railroad station and watch the arrival of the T&T.

The Beatty Indians in the 1920s and 1930s

During the 1920s and 1930s, there was an Indian camp in Beatty located on the east side of the railroad tracks, sheltered in cottonwood trees along the river. The majority of the approximately 15 families living there were Shoshone; they represented bands from throughout western Nevada and eastern California, including Death Valley, Lone Pine, and Bishop. Some came from as far away as Elko. Their homes were makeshift and had no plumbing. Water was carried in buckets from an outlet across the tracks belonging to the railroad (T. Cottonwood, 1987; Gillette, 1987).

Prior to the Depression, many of the Indians worked for the railroads that served the area and some helped construct Scotty's Castle. In the 1930s it was reported that a high percentage were employed by the Works Progress Administration. When that program ended and the railroads folded, the community disbanded and members did not return. Indeed, the camp was usually deserted during the summer as families went their various ways to cooler areas. Some visited relatives; others would migrate to camps in the surrounding mountains (T. Cottonwood, 1987; Gillette, 1987).

For several weeks in the fall, beginning in late September, the Indians in the Beatty area were involved in harvesting pine nuts. During that time, the Beatty school would be virtually deserted of Indian children. The Indians camped at traditional spots in the mountains and picked pine nuts for as long as two months. The first pine nuts were roasted in the cone in a large, bowl-like structure made of dried brush. A ceremony was performed and the bowl set on fire. Pine nuts were stored in sacks for use later in the winter months (T. Cottonwood, 1987; Gillette, 1987).

Conclusion

Between 1920 and 1940, Beatty was the economic hub of a vast area stretching from Sarcobatus Flat in the north to Ash Meadows in the south and from Death Valley on the west to the Lincoln county line on the east. Although the town experienced little growth, residents were able to earn their living by working for the railroad, owning and working in local businesses and small mining operations, and being employed in local and state government. It was a friendly community— everyone knew and respected each other. Still very much isolated, in many ways Beatty remained a small frontier town—a frontier oasis. Except for the automobile, it was scarcely indistinguishable from many communities found in the American West fifty years earlier.

CHAPTER 6

From World War II to 1960

he period from World War II to 1960 was a time of transformation for the town of Beatty. Though the total population changed little and the town's physical appearance remained relatively the same as it had been prior to the war, economic changes took place that would significantly impact the community's future. With the exception of Crowells' fluorspar mine, whose product was judged necessary for the war effort by federal authorities and thus remained open, the government's closure of gold mines in the area during World War II brought a permanent end to underground mining throughout the Beatty area.

Coinciding with the demise of underground mining came the increased and permanent presence of federal defense-related activities in the local economy with the establishment of Nellis Air Force Range in 1940 and the Nevada Test Site in 1950. Moreover, the establishment of Death Valley as a national monument in 1933 and Nevada's legalization of gambling in 1931 set the stage for the emergence of the town as a tourist center. Although tourism's impact was slow in developing, the town became increasingly oriented around servicing automobiles and providing food and lodging to highway travelers and the ever-increasing number of visitors to Death Valley. The rapid emergence of Las Vegas as a world-renowned tourism center was a major stimulus to Beatty; Beatty became a tiny tourist satellite to the glamorous city. Through it all, however, Beatty remained a small town, one in which face-to-face social relations prevailed, where serious crime was rare, and where people cared about each other.

Growth and Change After World War II

The population of the Beatty area nearly tripled between 1930 and 1950. In 1929, the population was 169. By 1940, the population of the Beatty township, extending from Lathrop Wells to Springdale, was 450; some of the growth was the result of activity at Carrara. Beatty weathered the Carrara shutdown, which followed the bombing of Pearl Harbor, and in 1950 the population was 485 ("Beatty Shows Population Growth in Past Decade," 1950). Perhaps reflecting needs pent up during the war, water demand in Beatty tripled between 1946 and 1947. The Reverts' power company had difficulty filling new requests for electric meters. In late 1947, a new power unit was installed by the Reverts, which increased community power by 50 percent ("New Unit to Up Power Capacity by 50 Per Cent," 1947). "Beatty may not be the fastest-growing town in Nevada (and then again it may)," the *Beatty Bulletin* stated in 1947, with unashamed hyperbole; but, it continued, there was "no denying that it's far more heavily populated than it was a year or two ago" ("Signs of Greater Prosperity Seen," 1947).

In the 1946 general election there were 266 eligible voters in Beatty, Ash Meadows, and Pahrump. In the 1948 election, there were 279 registered voters in Beatty alone—197 Democrats, 68 Republicans, 8 nonpartisans, 2 independents, and 4 undeclared—more than in all of southern Nye County in 1946. Ash Meadows and Pahrump added another 97 voters in 1948. In the 1948 general election, Robert Revert, youngest son of Henrietta and Albert Revert, was handily re-elected Beatty constable, and Dewey beat Truman in the Beatty area despite the Democrats' edge in registered voters ("District Voting Power Shows Increase of 39 Per Cent," 1948; "Beatty Supports Its Candidates," 1948).

In 1952 the number of registered voters in Beatty had fallen to 211, with an additional 18 in Ash Meadows and 80 in Pahrump; by 1954 the figure dropped to 204, about 11 percent of all Nye County voters. Spirits in town were high, however. In 1950, a New Jersey columnist wrote, after a short visit to Beatty, that despite its relatively small size the town was "more lively than Los Angeles and Hollywood put together!" ("East Coast Columnist Terms Beatty Livelier than LA and Hollywood," 1950).

Beatty experienced many changes during and after World War II. At the outset of the war, the federal government shut down all of the gas stations in town except for the Union Oil outlet; it also closed down all nonessential mining operations, which included gold and silver mines. Because fluorspar was essential in the production of steel, the Crowell Mine was allowed to operate; in fact, production was expanded. The war led to a severe shortage of manpower in Beatty. Many able-bodied men volunteered for military service and others were drafted (J. I. and D. Crowell, 1987; J. and M-K. Crowell, 1987; R. and C. Lisle, 1987).

Miners were not drafted, however, and sometimes miners were actually demobilized from the armed forces in order to work at essential mining operations. Ralph Lisle, who knew the mining trade, was not drafted until near the end of World

War II, and his experiences may have been typical of many miners. As one involved in an essential industry, for a time, he worked a small tungsten mine above Panamint City in the Panamint Mountains. He lived in the old ghost town and walked 2 miles up a narrow old wagon road every day to his diggings and then back to his lodging at the end of the day. The entire operation ran on hand labor. Lisle drilled the holes for blasting, using hand steel and a single jack; he hauled tungsten ore—considered an essential mineral by the government—down the trail on a half dozen burros to Panamint City, where it could be trucked down Surprise Canyon and out through the old ghost town of Ballarat on the west side of the Panamints.

One afternoon a flash flood caused by a heavy downpour on Telescope Peak sent a 20-foot wall of water roaring down Surprise Canyon, almost sweeping away to certain death Phil Lisle (Ralph's brother), Lottie Mills (his mother-in-law), and Sam Colvin (his brother-in-law). Seeing the wall of mud and water coming at them, they left the truck, climbed up the bank, and narrowly escaped. The water moved with such force that a boulder the size of a modern living room was washed a quarter of a mile down the canyon. Occurring as it did in the remote desert country, the flash flood went unnoticed except by the Lisles and their companions. Had it occurred in a populated area it would have been a disaster, with headlines worldwide.

Following his stay at Panamint City, Lisle, as an experienced miner, was sent by the government to work in a mine in Bishop, California, and later in the magnesium mine at Gabbs, Nevada. He was drafted in 1944 and served in Europe (R. and C. Lisle, 1987).

In October 1940, more than a year before Pearl Harbor and the official entry of the United States into World War II, the

U.S. government established the Tonopah Army Air Base and the Las Vegas Bombing and Gunnery Range (later renamed Nellis Air Force Range) on a vast area of land east of Beatty. Weather stations were placed around the range. Though there were a number of productive grazing, mining, and homestead claims on the newly restricted area, its closure did not represent a large economic loss for the town of Beatty. However, it was more than a decade before action was taken by the Air Force to compensate individuals for the privately owned lands and mineral and grazing rights that had been reserved for the 3-million-acre Las Vegas Bombing and Gunnery Range in Nye, Clark, and Lincoln counties. Prior to compensation most of the land had been leased by its owners to the Air Force for $1 a year or a similar nominal figure ("Air Force Seeks to Buy Rights on Bomb Range," 1953).

When the war was over, most Beatty residents expected life to return to normal. It never did. Mining in the Beatty area did not return to its pre–World War II level, and the era of the small, underground mine ended forever. The deathblow had been dealt during the war: Scrap metal was very valuable, and mines that had been closed were scavenged for their track, pipe, engines, hoists, and compressors. Large machinery that was too heavy to move was dynamited and broken into smaller pieces. Most of the mines had not been highly profitable to begin with, and any effort to reopen them following the war necessitated a reinvestment in track, pipe, and machinery, which could not be justified. In addition, men were no longer being trained as hard-rock miners, and in time, fewer and fewer men had the skill and knowledge to operate small, underground mines (J. and M-K. Crowell, 1987; R. and C. Lisle, 1987).

In 1947, the community took a great deal of pride in the new mill that was to be constructed on the hill west of the

Beatty Narrows near the site of the old town of Gold Center. Plans were made to construct a 20-ton pilot mill to treat ore from the Senator Stewart Mine in Bullfrog, then being leased by Homer Weeks ("Quinn Plans Pilot Mill to Test Ore," 1947). O. H. "Bud" Quinn and Clyde Barcus, along with Weeks, had the mill in operation by mid-1948 ("Mill Tests to Start Next Week," 1948; Weeks, 1987). There was also a good deal of discussion at this time regarding the important role the production of pumice, perlite, bentonite, and, of course, fluorspar—all nonmetallics—would have in Beatty's future economy. None except fluorspar ever proved to be more than a supplement to the economy, however.

Law Enforcement

Though sparsely populated, Nye County (which is larger than many states) presents challenges for law enforcement officers. The southern part of the county, a vast area lying south of the Esmeralda County line on U.S. Highway 95, traditionally was under the authority of the Beatty deputy. This area included the communities of Beatty, Amargosa Valley (including Ash Meadows), and Pahrump.

William H. "Bill" Thomas was the Nye County sheriff for nearly four decades, from 1917 until 1958 (with one two-year hiatus between 1919 and 1921). Sheriff Thomas, who has been described as easy-going, lived in Tonopah throughout his Nye County law enforcement career. At one point early in his career he ran for sheriff as a Socialist but was beaten. He ran again as an Independent and was elected (R. Revert, 1988).

For many years the Beatty deputy (who served under the sheriff) was elected in the Beatty township. I. B. Southey held the position of Beatty deputy for many years, until about 1930.

His career was successful, but an incident that occurred not long before he retired bothered him deeply. Southey responded to a call from the Gold Ace Bar in Beatty, and when he entered the bar, a man pulled a gun on him. Southey responded by drawing his own gun and he killed the man. Subsequent investigation revealed that the man's gun was not loaded (R. Revert, 1988).

John Vignolo, a highly regarded member of the community, was elected deputy sheriff of the Beatty area about 1930 and served until 1946. He served under Bill Thomas, the Nye County sheriff. Described as a "ranch type," Vignolo raised some cattle in Oasis Valley south of the hot springs.

Though Vignolo, a big man, seldom brought force to bear on a situation, when he thought it necessary, he was not afraid to move in on a crowd and deal physically with lawbreakers and ruffians (R. Revert, 1988). He carried a Colt Frontier model under his shirt, but he seldom had to draw it. Vignolo had his own priorities in law enforcement. In general, he did not go out of his way to attend to a case unless it happened to come his way, and he ordinarily did not respond to automobile accidents (R. Revert, 1988).

Generally, Vignolo had a laid-back approach, suited more to life in a small, face-to-face community of that time period than to today's crime-laden society. Jack Crowell recalls the time some Indian children entered his father's home in Beatty and stole a gun. Irving Crowell told Vignolo and Vignolo went to the Indians, retrieved the gun, and returned it to Crowell. Vignolo probably gave the children a good lecture, but that was the end of the matter. A similar incident today would result in reports, conferences between law enforcement officials, juvenile authorities, lawyers, judges, parents, and perhaps even the filling of charges. In contrast, Vignolo handled the problem and members of the community continued to live in relative peace (J. Crowell, 1991).

Vignolo and his predecessor, Southey, ignored the bootlegging that went on in southern Nye County during Prohibition. (Vignolo is said to have made a little booze himself.) It is reported that even the Pro-his (federal agents) gave Ash Meadows a wide berth. The area was said to be a bad place for strangers, and one federal agent did disappear in Ash Meadows. His car was found, but not the agent—nor any of his other belongings. Once during that era, when Vignolo was testifying in court in Tonopah, he responded to the question of where he was at the time of the incident: "I was in a bootleg joint playing solo," he said with a straight face. In his later years, he moved off his small cattle operation in Oasis Valley and resided in a house in town next to J. Irving and Dorothy Crowell. After retiring, he moved to the Modesto, California, area (R. Revert, 1988).

Robert Revert was elected Beatty deputy in 1946. At that time the position of constable (an officer of the justice court who served warrants) was consolidated with that of deputy. When Revert assumed the position, Nye County Sheriff William Thomas told him, "You'll have no soft time of it. I consider Ash Meadows to be the worst part of this county" as far as law enforcement is concerned. Revert realized that being responsible for law and order over such a vast rural area meant the work was never done: "You met yourself coming back on this job" (R. Revert, 1988).

Once on the job, Revert realized that as the law enforcement officer, he would have to set his priorities. Sheriff Thomas had given him full authority, and Revert placed high priority on automobile thefts, which were rampant at the time. His department apprehended numerous automobile thieves who attempted to drive stolen vehicles through the vast stretches of southern Nye County.

Problems were also encountered with indigents and derelicts migrating through southern Nevada. Revert described his policy with such drifters, known to local law enforcement people as "floaters": Those who caused trouble were informed that it would "be a good idea" if they moved along. If they did not heed this warning, they would be arrested and given a ten-day jail sentence. The sentence was then suspended, and they were put on their honor to work at a county job for the ten days. They usually disappeared within a day or two, perhaps to turn up at a later date and undergo the same process. It was also the custom of law enforcement officials who were roughed up by a prisoner during arrest or transportation to treat the prisoner similarly once he was in jail (R. Revert, 1988).

While Vignolo was the deputy, Judge William Gray was the justice of the peace in Beatty. Gray had lived in Rhyolite and was a long-time resident of the area. Gray's son, Howard, who grew up in Rhyolite, became a prominent Nevada attorney and legal counsel for Kennecott Copper in Ely. It is said that Howard and the judge once were discussing a local case. "Dad, you can't do that. That law's been changed," Howard said.

Judge Gray responded, "Well, I'm just using the old one [in this case]" (R. Revert, 1988).

Judge Gray was succeeded by Lawrence Kimball as Beatty justice of the peace. Kimball was a member of the family that operated the Kimball Brothers Stage Line in Rhyolite. About 1942, R. P. "Dick" Alyard, who was the proprietor of the local blacksmith shop, became the Beatty justice of the peace and served for a few years.

The Old Town Hall

For many years the Old Town Hall served as the social center of Beatty. Located on the corner of Third and Montgomery Street, it was a huge, marvelous, L-shaped frame building with a ceiling lined with pressed tin. A scroll on the front indicated the year it was built: 1906. Originally the Miners' Union Hall in Rhyolite, the building had been put together from two others.

Weddings and school functions were held in the Old Town Hall. The wing of the building also served as the beginning of the Beatty Library, starting about 1960. Carpet was laid and bookshelves were built; it served as the community's library until the Fleischmann Foundation provided funds to build a new library, housed in a geodesic dome on Ward and Fourth Street (J. and M-K. Crowell, 1987).

When Beatty constructed a new community center in the 1960s, the Old Town Hall was torn down. Harry Johnson paid for the privilege of demolishing it. He salvaged some lovely old timbers, some as long as 30 feet and almost completely free of knots. Such timbers would be quite expensive now because of the scarcity of such quality and the difficulty of hauling them on a truck. They were, of course, originally brought to Rhyolite on the railroad. In the finest tradition of cannibalizing one desert building for another, Harry Johnson used some of those timbers in the construction of his own home (J. and M-K. Crowell, 1987).

Frank and Edith Brockman recalled the Meander Inn, a program of the mid-1950s that was housed in the Old Town Hall. The program provided an opportunity for local teens to gather and dance. Kenneth Priest was the guiding light of the program. People over 21 were not admitted, and teens were reimbursed for records they purchased and brought to the inn, which ensured that the music was current and popular (F. and E. Brockman, 1987).

Bert Lemmon's Beatty Theater

Bert Lemmon, who had graduated from Beatty High School in 1940, returned from the Army in 1946. Soon after, he found a 1920s vintage Cineflex 35-mm projector stored in a closet in the Old Town Hall. Lemmon had a number of contacts in the film industry in Los Angeles, and he decided to use those contacts for the benefit of Beatty and Death Valley residents.

It was common in the film industry in the 1940s for movies to be held over in theaters if they proved to be popular. When a film was held over for a week or longer, it meant that a movie previously scheduled had to be held back until the run of the holdover was finished. Through his contacts, Lemmon was able to have some of the movies being held back in Los Angeles shipped to Beatty by bus. He then showed them in the Old Town Hall before they were seen in Los Angeles. Feature films were shown in Beatty on Wednesday and Saturday nights and in Furnace Creek earlier in the week.

The projector was housed in a loft that was only accessible through a trap door. The screen was approximately 10 feet square; there were 24 padded seats and the rest were wooden. Lemmon recalled with a chuckle that dogs would sometimes enter the theater while a movie was being shown. If a Western was playing and a stampede was under way, the dogs would rush to the stage and begin barking at the cattle (R. and C. Lisle, 1987).

Motels: Beatty Puts Out the Welcome Mat

During the 1930s there were few accommodations for tourists or travelers in Beatty. The old Gold Ace Bar had a few rooms but they were mainly for the bar's hired help. The same was probably true of the Exchange Club. The Montgomery Hotel, the finest hotel in the Beatty region, had long since been moved to Pioneer (it eventually burned down). There were a few accommodations available at the Beatty Hotel and across the street at the Mayflower Hotel. (From 1963 to 1967 the Beatty Hotel was owned by Bill Cragg and was called the Cragg Hotel) (J. and M-K. Crowell, 1987).

The first modern motel in Beatty, El Portal, was built at the west end of town on the road to Daylight Pass by a man named Jim Staley in the late 1930s. Originally El Portal was an auto court with rooms and adjoining garages, but the garages were later converted into rooms. Prior to the construction of El Portal, travelers who broke down on the highway or were otherwise stranded often stayed with local families until repairs could be made (J. and M-K. Crowell, 1987).

In 1947 and 1948, there was a great deal of building and improvements in Beatty's accommodations. In April 1947, Charles H. Dodge of Grand Rapids, Michigan, opened his "ultra modern" Gateway Trailer Park at the north end of town on land purchased from the Reverts ("New Beatty Trailer Park Composite of 'The Best,'" 1947). A month later plans were announced to add seven new units to El Portal, whose name had been changed to the Bullfrog Motel ("Bullfrog to Add Seven New Units," 1947). In 1948, the Bates family purchased the Bullfrog Motel and the original name (El Portal) was restored ("Bates Family Purchases Spacious Bullfrog Motel," 1948). That same year Dodge sold the Gateway to Bid Porter, former owner of the Cook Ranch ("Disclose Sale of Gateway Trailer Park to Porter," 1948); and ground was broken by V. E. Elliot of Long Beach, California, for a 12-unit motel—the Wagonwheel—at the junction of Highways 95 and 58, where the Gold Ace Bar had stood before it burned down ("Construction of 12-Unit Motel Launched by Epps," 1948).

Some years after El Portal was built, Hank Melcher built the Amargosa River Inn (originally called Hank's Motel) at the corner of Beach and Main—the former site of a small Standard station just south of Richings' store. The Burro Inn, Stagecoach, Lori Motel, and Brockmans' Desert Inn (which was built along Highway 95 approximately across from the Burro Inn) are all of more recent vintage (J. and M-K. Crowell, 1987).

For several decades, travel at night on Highway 95 north of Beatty could be dangerous, particularly for tourists, truck drivers, and others who did not know the area. The roadway was not fenced, and cattle and burros often wandered onto the highway. Many tragic accidents occurred when drivers collided with animals in the darkness. During the mid-1980s, Highway 95 was fenced on the north, which helped solve the problem (J. and M-K. Crowell, 1987).

Raising Cattle in the Beatty Area

Beatty is not cattle country. Residents like to point out that it is "10–30 country," meaning that a cow needs a mouth 10 feet wide and the ability to run 30 miles an hour to get enough food to stay alive (J. and M-K. Crowell, 1987). John Delfs did raise a few cattle for many years on his ranch on the Amargosa just south of Beatty toward the Narrows, but later he sold out to Bid Porter. Porter ran cattle and a few horses in the hills west of Beatty, where a number of springs can be found, as far as

Hooligan Springs at the foot of the Grapevine Mountains. Others have maintained a few cattle on small ranches in the grassy areas to the north in Oasis Valley toward Springdale and also in the flats between the highway north of Beatty and the Grapevine Mountains. Pasture in the area is limited, however, and these operations have never been large (J. and M-K. Crowell, 1987; A. Revert, 1987).

Prostitution

Some Beatty residents, like many rural Nevadans, are sensitive to outsiders' criticism of the legal operation of houses of prostitution in and near their communities. Supporters are quick to emphasize that legalized prostitution is a safe relationship for both the prostitutes and their clients—safer than illegal street prostitution. They also note that making prostitution illegal does not eliminate it. Those who oppose regulated prostitution are asked, "Who does it harm?"

During the 1930s there were two houses of prostitution in Beatty: the Willow Tree and the Red Rooster. They were next door to each other at the edge of town—across the street from where the swimming pool was later built. Prostitutes were generally tolerated in town as long as they did not become a nuisance and no one complained. But in the late 1950s, complaints by a minority concerning the brothels' presence led to their closure by the sheriff's office. Other town residents protested the closure, which led to nationwide newspaper publicity (J. and M-K. Crowell, 1987).

Soon after the brothels in town were closed, similar establishments were opened on the outskirts of Beatty. Joe Conforte, who became the owner of the well-known Mustang Ranch in northern Nevada, opened the Jolly Dolly, later known as Fran's Star Ranch, just north of town. For a time there was a brothel known as the Blue Goose near the airport on the south side of town (J. and M-K. Crowell, 1987; Weeks, 1987).

Unlike most brothel owners, Fran York, who eventually took over and renamed Fran's Star Ranch, maintained a visible profile in the community. (Other madams and prostitutes were rarely seen in town, and when they were they seldom "recognized" the local citizenry on the streets.) But Fran became famous in southern Nevada for her charitable activities in town. The town, in turn, did not ignore her when adversity hit. When her establishment burned down in the late 1970s, a benefit dance was held and funds were raised to help put her back in business (J. and M-K. Crowell, 1987).

A Trip to Las Vegas

In the mid-1940s, most Beatty residents looked forward to a trip to town—that is, to Las Vegas. The Crowell boys, Jack and Don, were no exceptions. At that time there was no speed limit on Nevada's rural highways, and most people drove 65 or 70 miles per hour, so the trip took two hours or a little less.

Las Vegas was small and centered along a few blocks on Fremont Street. The Crowells always had a grocery list to fill at Sewell's (later the Market Spot). Electrical and plumbing supplies were purchased at Standard Wholesale, automotive parts at Clark County Wholesale. There was usually a trip to Woitishek Lumber Company or Von Tobel's for lumber needs. Sears was at Sixth and Fremont. Shopping was so convenient that it seldom took more than two or three hours. Lunch—a hamburger and a milkshake—was enjoyed at Smith's near Third and Stewart Avenue and usually followed by a movie at El Portal or the Palace. The Crowell boys would be out of the movie by 3:00 or 4:00 in the afternoon, and the family usually arrived home by 6:00 (J. and M-K. Crowell, 1987).

The *Beatty Bulletin*

On April 25, 1947, after a hiatus of nearly 40 years, Beatty once again had a newspaper, or at least part of one. Robert A. Crandall, editor of the *Goldfield News*, began to devote a section of his paper to the news of Beatty under a special heading: *Beatty Bulletin*. This section ran until December 28, 1956, when Crandall merged the *Goldfield News* with the *Tonopah Times-Bonanza*. The *Beatty Bulletin* started out strongly as a source of advertising and news on Beatty, but it slowly faded. In its last years it came to contain as much news on Nye County generally as on Beatty.

The Nevada Test Site

In mid-January 1951, the Atomic Energy Commission (AEC), predecessor of the U.S. Department of Energy, announced that atomic tests would begin on the 5000-square-mile bombing and gunnery range located directly east of Beatty. Initially there was considerable speculation among the southern Nevada residents regarding the exact location of the site of the tests ("Speculation Rife on Exact Location of Nuclear Tests," 1951). There were indications that the first blast would be set off northeast of Beatty on the other side of 7428-foot Timber Mountain ("To Conduct Atomic Tests Near Here," 1951; "Beatty Appears to Be Nearest Town to Site of Atomic Tests," 1951). The Nevada atomic experiments, it was announced, were being designed to "save precious time" in perfecting atomic warfare, including "experimental nuclear explosions for the development of so-called A-bombs." Tests related to the development of atomic warheads for artillery shells and guided missiles were among the chief objectives ("Beatty Appears to Be Nearest Town . . . ," 1951).

Local residents were assured that the tests presented no

hazards and that "all necessary precautions . . . will be undertaken to insure the maintenance of safety conditions" ("Beatty Appears to Be Nearest Town . . . ," 1951). An article in the *Beatty Bulletin* stated:

> A spokesman for the atomic energy commission emphasizes that tall canyons will ring the nuclear experimental explosions, providing an effective shield against transmittal of radio-activity beyond the controlled area. . . .
>
> There is a good likelihood that residents of this section, particularly around Beatty, will not only hear the detonations but will be within visual range of the familiar mushroom type cloud caused by the explosion of atomic weapons ("Beatty Appears to Be Nearest Town . . . ," 1951).

Yet, despite assurances by the AEC, that same issue of the *Beatty Bulletin* carried an account of remarks by Frank H. Bartholomew, vice president of United Press and witness to the atomic explosions at Hiroshima and Nagasaki. He emphasized that atomic explosions had previously been "highly unpredictable." He said, "The only safe assumption is that the atomic energy commission doesn't know what will happen . . . and has scheduled the physical tests to find out" ("Atomic Explosions Are Unpredictable, Writes Witness of Two Blasts," 1951). On January 27, 1951, the first atomic weapon was tested over Frenchman Flat (Titus, 1986:56).

To many Beatty residents, the tests were more of a curiosity than anything else. The shots were usually set off early in the dim light of dawn, and many locals gathered to watch them. To reach a favorite viewing spot, residents went south on Highway 95 to a point about 2 miles south of where U.S. Ecology is located, then turned back to the northeast on a dirt road near the vicinity of the Sterling and Saga mines. There, at the top of a saddle, spectators could look straight out over the Test Site to Yucca Flat, a distance of about 30 miles (J. and M-K. Crowell, 1987).

The sight of an atomic explosion in the first light of dawn is remembered as thrilling by some Beatty residents. One instant there was darkness; the next second there was blue-white light. The light rapidly expanded and then contracted to almost nothing. Then the orange fireball started to build, the colors faded into purples, and the huge mushroom cloud formed. Usually there was no sound except for a faint rumbling, like thunder, in the distance. Jack Crowell remembered that once near the end of an atmospheric test, the desert winds seemed to shape the giant mushroom cloud into the form of a huge question mark (J. and M-K. Crowell, 1987).

In October 1951, the Atomic Energy Commission announced that a new set of atomic tests would be undertaken at Frenchman Flat proving ground. The AEC warned that "a condition might develop at mines and ranches quite close to the site that would make it advisable to move residents for a few hours" ("New Atom Jolt Brewing!" 1951). On April 22, 1952, there was a "king-sized atomic detonation at nearby Frenchman Flat" ("Yesterday's Atomic Jolt Clearly Seen, Heard, Felt Here," 1952). The flash from the blast was clearly visible at 9:30 A.M. and was heard and felt in Beatty. "The sodden boom of the explosion rolled through town within five minutes after the blast," and both the impact and sound were "very distinct," reported the *Beatty Bulletin* editor, Pauline Terrell ("Yesterday's Atomic Jolt . . . ," 1952). The device was dropped from a high-flying aircraft, and there was a simulated paratroop drop and land invasion by ground troops in the wake of the explosion. The telltale grayish mushroom cloud, framed with pink at its periphery, rose after the explosion ("Yesterday's Atomic Jolt . . . ," 1952).

In early December 1952, the AEC indicated that yet another series of tests would be under way in the spring and that one of the purposes would be to determine the effects of nuclear blasts on an "actual city." The commission announced its intention to build a "typical" city near Beatty for the experiment. Later that month the AEC announced that Reynolds Electric and Engineering Company of El Paso, Texas, had been awarded a three-part contract for maintenance, minor construction of scientific structures, and support services for the AEC's Nevada Proving Grounds, as the facility was sometimes called ("To Build 'Typical' City Near Here for A-Tests," 1952; "Reynolds Concern Gets Proving Ground Pact," 1952). In January it was also reported that the spring tests would include 20-ton cannons hurling atomic missiles for the first time ("To Resume Atomic Tests Near Beatty in March," 1953). In March 1953, the AEC issued a warning to "ranchers, miners, migrants, private fliers and others concerned" that another series of nuclear experiments was ready to begin, emphasizing that the "Nevada Atomic Proving Grounds" was closed to all unauthorized personnel ("AEC Issues Warnings as Atomic Tests Near," 1953).

The *Beatty Bulletin* also carried an item that month detailing the AEC's efforts to protect people in the vicinity of the Nevada Proving Grounds. It described efforts to monitor radiation before and during nuclear tests both at the proving grounds and in an area within a 200-mile radius of the Test Site ("AEC Moves to Protect Persons in this Area," 1953). By March 1953, a total of 453 damage claims had been filed against the Atomic Energy Commission in connection with its testing in Nevada. All but 27 of those claims were sustained in connection with two series of tests in 1951 ("Atomic Damage Claims Decline," 1953).

In April 1953, a U.S. Air Force B-50 bomber dropped an

atomic device that was detonated more than 5000 feet above the Yucca Flat target area at 7:30 in the morning. Because of the height of the blast, traffic along Highway 95 was cautioned to stop a few minutes before the detonation. Few people in the Beatty area, however, were able to see the blast because of the brightness of the rising sun along their line of sight ("Few See Flash from Big Burst," 1953).

In October 1955, it was announced that Los Alamos Scientific Laboratories would use the Nevada Test Site in November for a series of experiments to determine the safety of various nuclear devices in the event of accidents, including fires during hauling and storage ("'Small' Nuclear Tests in Store," 1955).

For years Nevada Test Site officials have provided miners in the Beatty area with advance information on scheduling of all but the smallest tests. As a precaution, safety officials and miners do not want to be underground when the tests are conducted. Though Rainier Mesa is not visible from the Crowell Mine, following large shots in the 1970s, dust was sometimes seen to rise from the mesa (J. and M-K. Crowell, 1987).

Beatty is generally upwind from the test area, and radiation fallout from testing has never been seen as a major problem in the community as it was for residents more likely to be living downwind from ground zero, such as those in Railroad and Reveille valleys to the north, Alamo in the Pahranagat Valley in Lincoln County, and St. George, Utah, to the east. Moreover, Beatty residents have been trustful of the government on nuclear matters, and the majority believe that their trust has been justified. Most admit decades later that they are much less naive regarding nuclear testing than they were in the early years of Test Site operation. The vast majority of Beatty residents said they see no real harm in the community from testing (A. Revert, 1987).

During the summer of 1951, there was considerable discussion about the effect testing and the construction it required would have on employment in the area. It was reported that 300 construction workers were then employed at the Test Site, with a maximum anticipated construction force of 1300. By July, seven construction contracts had been let and three more were in the bidding process. These contracts included the construction of permanent facilities at a camp for testing personnel, administrative and operational structures, technical installations, and access roads and fencing, along with various utilities. Efforts were made by the AEC to determine the availability of local labor from southern Nevada, and any eventual need for workers from outside the region ("To Employ 1300 at Atomic Test Site," 1951).

Employment opportunities at the Test Site resulted in an influx of new families into Beatty beginning in 1951. As a result, housing was at a premium. A number of Test Site families moved to Beatty and sent their children to the local schools. Rents in Beatty, despite the housing shortage, were said to be lower than in Las Vegas. Local businesses reported a noticeable increase in sales. There was talk of an access road between the Test Site and Springdale on Highway 95 and also of a railroad spur line to the Test Site with a right-of-way passing through or near Beatty ("Influx of New Families Taxes Beatty's Housing," 1951). There was also some speculation that the old Tonopah air base would be reactivated as a Strategic Air Command base ("Survey May Presage Air Base Reactivation," 1951).

Through the years the residents of Beatty have borne nuclear testing in their neighborhood with good humor. From the outset residents of Beatty have been employed at the Test Site. However, given the community's proximity to the testing facility, local employment at the Test Site has never been as high as early speculation had predicted and not up to what many considered a fair proportion. Though residents in the Beatty area continue to be among the "best friends" that the Test Site has in Nevada, many feel that federal officials have dragged their feet for years on the employment issue (J. and M-K. Crowell, 1987). One resident summed up the relationship between Beatty and the Test Site: "It's been a good thing for Beatty. It has proved employment for a lot of people, a lot of our friends. Probably a lot of people we know and live with as friends wouldn't even be here if it were not for the Test Site" (J. and M-K. Crowell, 1987).

The presence of the Test Site has meant contracts for a few Beatty businesses. Beginning in 1951, the Revert brothers operated the first oil distributorship on the Test Site; they supplied petroleum products to the federal government and also to Test Site contractors. Robert Revert remembered his efforts—in the days when he was in charge of site security— to have workers who lived on the Test Site buy Nye County automobile plates. His success added to Nye County's slim tax coffers (R. Revert, 1988).

Another benefit to Beatty and to Nye County is the contribution made to the tax base by contractors working on the Test Site. Prior to the 1960s Nye County was poor; funds were always short. A lawsuit instituted in the mid-1960s by Nye County and supported by Clark County was brought to force contractors working on federal property to pay county taxes (R. Revert, 1988; Neighbors, 1988).

The Nye County district attorney at the time, William P. Beko, and Roy Neighbors, a county deputy working in the Mercury area, did much of the research that provided the basis of the lawsuit. While captain of security at the Test Site, Robert Revert had a firsthand view of Beko's efforts to tax private property and contractors' equipment being used there.

Revert noted that Beko worked for years, without extra compensation, to tax the contractors. The Atomic Energy Commission fought the issue and put out a nationwide search for legal talent. Revert recalled the time that twenty high-powered attorneys from the AEC were gathered in the Nye County Courthouse in Tonopah to fight Beko.

> If ever a David and Goliath battle existed, that had to be it. If ever there was a hero for Nye County, it has to be Bill Beko. He is the one individual who has done more for Nye County than anybody else. I don't care who you talk about, Pat McCarran, Brougher, Pittman, or anybody else. Single-handedly, he has done more for Nye County than any other person in the whole state, ever! (R. Revert, 1988).

Beko and Nye County won the suit. The case was ruled on by the Nevada Supreme Court in 1970, and the county's right to tax the property and equipment of private contractors working for the federal government on the Nevada Test Site and similar facilities was confirmed (R. Revert, 1988; Neighbors, 1988).

With money from the taxes, the county has been able to undertake many projects that previously had been impossible. Nye County, for example, used part of the money to pay cash for the construction of a high school in Pahrump. Over the years, Test Site contractors have also made available to nearby communities and groups considerable amounts of surplus equipment at minimal charge. For example, much of the electrical and plumbing supplies used in the construction of Beatty's Water and Sanitation District and in local park and recreation projects originated as surplus equipment on the Test Site (J. and M-K. Crowell, 1987).

The local population also became involved with law enforcement of the vast Test Site facility. Law enforcement on the site has long been the responsibility of the Nye County Sheriff's Office, with the captain in charge being appointed by the Nye County sheriff. By 1960, there was a staff of four law enforcement officers on the Test Site, with Hugh Moran in charge. Upon ending his career as Beatty's Nye County deputy, Bob Revert began working at the Test Site; he thought he would only be filling in temporarily for officers on vacation. Before Revert knew it, however, he was in charge of the office. He found that law enforcement needs could not be met with a staff of only four deputies, and he was given three additional ones. Jackass Flat was opened soon after that, and more deputies were eventually added to accommodate the increased population and traffic. The security force on the Test Site had grown to 26 in 1972, when Revert retired (R. Revert, 1988).

Law officers on the Test Site were responsible for a number of duties, including investigation of all traffic accidents. Because the Nevada Highway Patrol was understaffed, Test Site officials were also responsible for Highway 95 in the vicinity of the Test Site in Nye County. The section of Highway 95 between Mercury and Las Vegas was known as the "widow-maker." Revert remembered that in December 1961 there were eight fatalities on the Nye section alone. In addition, the deputies patrolled the many miles of road on the Test Site and worked under the FBI on those cases that needed attention. They also patrolled, for instance, the workers' camp and canteen in Area 12 on the Test Site. Revert remembered calculating the volume of beer and whiskey consumed at that canteen in the early 1960s: 132 gallons of beer and 18 gallons of whiskey in a single day (R. Revert, 1988).

Ralph Lisle: The Post–World War II Days

In 1953 Lisle's Union 76 station located on Second Street burned down ("Flames Destroy Lisle Garage, Gas Station,"

1953). A smaller version of the station was soon rebuilt, but when Highway 95 was widened through town, the new road was so close to the pumps that the station became impractical to operate. By 1955, Texaco Oil Company was interested in entering the Beatty service station market and helped Lisle construct a new station across the street—under the Texaco banner. In about 1960, the Lisles decided to remodel their home and Ralph purchased a truckload of lumber and building supplies in Reno and had it hauled to Beatty. As the rebuilding and remodeling proceeded, friends and neighbors asked if they could buy nails, small quantities of lumber, and other building supplies from his truckload. Lisle obliged and then replaced what he had sold. Supplying neighbors in this way gradually grew into a lumber and hardware business at the site originally occupied by his Union 76 station. During the mid-1950s, Lisle obtained a Goodyear Tire franchise; when Goodyear phased out, he switched to a Western Auto franchise and sold appliances along with the hardware (R. and C. Lisle, 1987; C. Lisle, 1989).

Ralph Lisle served as a Nye County commissioner for fourteen years—from 1950 to 1964. He first ran for the post because he believed that residents of southern Nye County needed someone to speak for them. Once he was a commissioner, he was surprised to discover how little money there actually was to run the county. He pointed out that in the mid-1980s annual county income exceeded the total assessed valuation of all the property in the county when he first became county commissioner.

During his tenure, he and his colleagues worked hard to improve county services. They were the first to pave county roads. Lisle also remembered with pride the upgrading of the Tonopah water system, which is controlled by Nye County. The old pipe from Ryepatch, made of wood and wrapped with wire, was replaced with a metal pipe. As Lisle recalled, the old pipe was more patches than pipe (R. and C. Lisle, 1987).

Robert Revert's Career as State Assemblyman

In the early 1950s, Nye County had two representatives in the State Assembly. One represented Tonopah and the other the remainder of Nye County. In 1951 the job of deputy-constable in Beatty was made an appointive position, and Robert Revert ran and was elected assemblyman from the Second District in Nye County. He ran again in 1953 and was re-elected. He declined to run in 1955; but he ran again and was re-elected in 1957, 1959, and 1961. While an assembly-man, Revert was involved in the passage of much gambling legislation, and he is particularly proud of laws that permit the allocation of some Nevada gambling monies by county. He was also instrumental in bringing a modern phone system to Beatty (R. Revert, 1988).

During Revert's time in the legislature, he explored the possibility of merging Esmeralda and Nye counties. Esmeralda County was quite poor; at times there was barely enough money to keep the street lights burning in Goldfield. Esmeralda was in favor of the merger, but Nye County officials were opposed. They felt that it would be a drain on the Nye tax base and would make an already large county even larger (R. Revert, 1988).

Revert was chairman of the Roads and Transportation Committee in the State Assembly, and he played an important role in arranging for paving the road from Las Vegas to Pahrump over Mountain Springs Pass in 1954. He also helped get all but the last 4 miles of the road from Gabbs to the Icythyosaur Park paved and was instrumental in getting improvements made to the gravel road between Tonopah and Gabbs (R. Revert, 1988).

Concerning his career as an assemblyman, Revert emphasized that there is no substitute for experience in the legislative process. Politics, he said, is a series of compromises; you hope to drive bargains and hope to come out with your share or maybe a little more. "Your legislator has to feel his way along for himself, and there is a lot of on-the-job training." When asked about the legislative process, Revert smiled, then quoted Mark Twain, who said there were two things a sensitive person should never watch being made: sausage and the law (R. Revert, 1988).

Conclusion

In 1960 Beatty was the largest community in Nye County south of Tonopah. Though it had become a part of the modern defense and tourist economy, it remained very much a frontier community in its values. Residents of Beatty might earn a living by working at the Nevada Test Site or by owning a gas station, but when it came to how they looked at the world, they probably had more in common with a Rhyolite prospector or miner than someone living in a similar-sized community in many other areas of the country. Then—as now—residents of Beatty loved the desert and its vastness; the town's geographic isolation, far from being a disadvantage, was seen as a precious asset. Residents took pride in their honesty and their desire to treat others as they wished to be treated—with fairness and dignity. Though they were dependent on the economic system that stretched far beyond Beatty, they cherished their independence and freedom from the rigidity and demands for conformity that other communities outside Nevada often imposed. In Beatty, as in much of Nevada, people were still free to be themselves, free to try to fill the biggest pair of shoes as long as they did not step on someone else's toes. In practice, big dreams did not usually become reality; but as with the old prospectors, the dream, as well as the possibility, was always there.

CHAPTER 7

The Modern Era: 1960 to the Present

eatty's infrastructure developed significantly in the early 1960s. New community sewer and water systems were constructed; new power lines brought electricity from Hoover Dam; and a new phone system was installed. Additionally, a spirit of modernism and community participation led to cooperative activities that benefited the entire community.

The Beatty Volunteer Fire Department

As in small towns everywhere, Beatty residents live with the threat of fire; in Nevada, however, the dry climate increases the threat. From the time the town was established through the 1950s, wooden structures that caught fire almost invariably burned to the ground. A major fire of the late 1930s or very early 1940s wiped out the Gold Ace Bar. The Gold Ace, a large, single-story building that featured a big dance floor and a bar, was across the street from the Exchange Bar (on the site later occupied by the Wagon Wheel Motel). "Bombo" Cottonwood, a young boy at the time, was in Tonopah attending a July 4 celebration. He recalled that the smoke from the fire could be seen in Tonopah, but "nobody knew what was going on until the mail truck came through" (T. Cottonwood, 1987). On his way back and forth to elementary school, Jack Crowell used to kick through the ashes of the Gold Ace Bar looking for melted coins from the slot machines that had been in the bar (J. Crowell, 1991).

Other fires took their toll. In 1947 fire wiped out Ray Moffet's laundry building ("Fire Truck Can't Reach Site of Blaze," 1947). In the 1950s, the wooden additions to the stone house at the old Beatty Ranch burned down; Ike Shaw was burned to death when his cabin went up in flames ("Ike Shaw Burned Fatally in Blaze," 1954). Gilbert Landis's house burned down in the late 1950s, as did a structure on Fred Davies's property prior to that. In 1953 Ralph Lisle's garage and gas station were wiped out by fire ("Flames Destroy Lisle Garage, Gas Station," 1953). The Mayflower Hotel, which was moved to Beatty from Pioneer (after that town folded), was later converted to apartments. The structure burned in 1972.

Beatty's first fire station, a building constructed of galvanized tin, was located on the north side of the Old Town Hall. In 1949 a building was moved from the Tonopah airport, placed on lots located at the corner of Montgomery and Third streets on the south side of the Old Town Hall; the lots were owned by the Beatty Improvement Association and the building served as the second fire station ("Fire Station Building to Be Moved to Beatty," 1949). A family lived in the back of a 20-x-60-foot building and maintained the station in exchange for rent (R. Lisle, C. Lisle, 1991). During this period the fire department was not well trained or well equipped, and state-of-the-art fire-fighting equipment was not purchased (Weeks, 1987). Beginning about 1961, a group of young, community-spirited residents decided to push for better equipment and training for Beatty's volunteer fire department. The third firehouse was made from cement blocks purchased by the county, mortar left over from the construction of Scotty's Castle, and other materials scrounged from the Test Site. It was built by volunteer labor. In 1970 when Nye County won its suit regarding taxing contractors at the Test Site, money from that suit bought a fire engine for the new firehouse. Constant pressure was successfully applied on the Nye County commissioners to acquire additional fire-fighting equipment.

The volunteer ambulance service was eventually incorporated into the fire department, and the Fleischmann Foundation contributed to the purchase of an ambulance. By the 1980s, the Beatty fire department was an efficient force. Buildings that in the past would have burned to the ground are now regularly saved. In a major fire in the Exchange Club, for example, in the winter of 1987, damage was limited to the upper story because of the effectiveness of the fire department (J. and M-K. Crowell, 1987).

Volunteer firemen make sacrifices to be members of the department. A fire occurs about, on average, every month or two. When the siren rings, volunteers roll out of bed or drop whatever they are doing to rush to the firehouse. They practice on weekends and also study and watch training films— activities that take them away from their families and leisure pursuits. Beatty residents take considerable, justified pride in their fire department. In the late 1980s, a state fire official told local representatives that if his home was on fire, he would rather have the Beatty volunteers at the scene than firemen from any of Nevada's largest cities, although he did not mean to demean city fire-fighting capabilities (J. and M-K. Crowell, 1987; Weeks, 1987).

Civic Improvements

Prior to the 1960s, Beatty lacked recreational facilities. What served as a "ballfield," an area of gravel and rocks, was the result of attempts to scrape the sagebrush off one corner of a lot. With no adequate field, students at the Beatty school could not play tackle football. There were limited options for children and adults who wanted to swim. They could splash in the cold water of a rancher's reservoir in Oasis Valley or travel to the Beatty Narrows, where there were some small natural pools. Aside from a small swimming pool at one of the local motels, the closest facility was at Renee Gibson's place above Springdale or in Death Valley, 40 miles away (J. and M-K. Crowell, 1987).

In 1965, community activists, led by Jack Crowell, decided to remedy the situation. They formed a Parks and Recreation Advisory Board and informed the Nye County commissioners of their desire for more recreational facilities in Beatty. The board's efforts eventually produced results. Ralph Lisle, who was chairman of the county commissioners, helped pass a 5 percent local room tax to help fund recreational projects. This tax enabled the town to guarantee that money would be available to maintain recreational facilities. With additional county monies, Beatty eventually constructed a football field; volunteers provided much of the labor. In 1973 Beatty High School fielded an eight-man football team. With the aid of county and state funds and a grant from the Fleischmann Foundation, Beatty opened its newly completed, large swimming pool in 1976. In 1989, the Parks and Recreation Advisory Board began work on a second ballfield, which is now completed. In summer 1991, a grassed golf driving range was built. None of these projects was accomplished easily; each was made possible only through the dedication and persistence of community volunteers (J. and M-K. Crowell, 1987).

Schools

When the Reverts moved to Beatty in 1930, young Robert attended school with the other children in an adobe building located behind the Exchange Club. During the 1930s, building materials were salvaged in Rhyolite, transported to Beatty, and a schoolhouse was constructed between Fourth and Irving on Montgomery Street, the site reserved for a school on the original plat map of the town. The building was still in use in 1991. Several other structures were added to form the school complex, including the old high school building. In the late 1950s and early 1960s, after two rejections by the voters, a bond issue for construction of additional school space was passed, and buildings to house an office, three classrooms, and the gym were added. Additional buildings were constructed in the late 1960s, and still later six more classrooms were constructed and a prefabricated building was assembled to serve as the shop and dressing room for the gym. In 1991, a new multi-million dollar high school was built for students from Beatty, Amargosa Valley, and Death Valley. The old school buildings are now used by children from the kindergarten through the eighth grade (J. Crowell, 1990). When John Delfs died in 1956, his will established a scholarship fund that granted $2000 to the outstanding graduate from Beatty High School each year ("$2000 Annual Scholarship Established by Delfs' Will," 1956).

Medical Care

For many years there was no medical care available in Beatty; the nearest physicians were located in Tonopah, more than 90 miles to the north, and Las Vegas, more than 110 miles to the south. One resident remarked, "Read the newspaper. They talk about a poor town some place in the Midwest that is 16 miles from a doctor. In rural Nye county, when you're 16 miles from [health care], you're close" (J. and M-K. Crowell, 1987). Doctors could be consulted over the phone after telephone service became available during World War II, but prior to that residents were extremely isolated from medical care.

In the 1920s there was a medical clinic in an office on Main Street. For a time during the 1950s, local medical offices were located in Judge Gray's old house, near the Episcopal Church. The physician held somewhat regular office hours in the judge's house. A few years later, land was donated for a clinic on Hospital Hill on the southernmost part of Irving Street. A mill and assay office had been located at the site, where ore from the Polaris Mine at Rhyolite was processed. The mill had been torn down during World War II, but the assay office was still standing. Volunteers added on to the old office to make a medical clinic. In about 1960, Anita Johnson, a registered nurse who had worked in a clinic, moved to town. Once people learned that she had some medical knowledge, she found herself putting ice on bumped heads and stitching up wounds. She eventually became the nurse-receptionist at the clinic and gained so much experience as Beatty's answer to a doctor that the University of Nevada Medical School consulted with her in developing its program for training nurse practitioners. Beginning in the early 1970s, physicians' assistants used the community medical center to treat local patients (J. and M-K. Crowell, 1987).

Churches

Rural Nevadans as a group have never been noted to be strongly religious. Yet for many, church and religious services have always played a vital role in their lives. It is not known exactly when the first European-based religious services were observed in Beatty, but it was certainly in the community's earliest days.

The Episcopal Church, a stone building on the corner of Third and Main, is the oldest religious structure in Beatty; it dates to a period prior to the 1920s. Beatty's Catholic Church was built in 1956 on Main Street between Third and Fourth. Father Sidney Raemers and military personnel in the area at the time are reported to have been the driving force behind the construction of the Catholic Church. It has always had mission status, and a priest from Tonopah holds services twice a month ("Beatty to Have Catholic Church," 1956).

The Beatty Community Church, located on 2-1/2 acres in the west part of town, was founded by the American Baptists and has an active following. In the mid-1980s Southern Baptists broke off from the Community Church and constructed their own church. There is also a Mormon Church located on the west edge of town.

Beatty residents also recalled a cult that started in the early 1980s and existed for a short period. Its appeal was mainly to the young, and it seemed to dominate their lives. One member of the cult had a vision that indicated Beatty was going to be the next Sodom and Gomorrah. The church moved to Las Vegas and then on to Oregon (J. and M-K. Crowell, 1987).

Formation of the Lions Club

Old-timers in Beatty remembered that for a short time in the 1930s, the community had a Lions Club. In 1959 a new Lions Club with over twenty members was chartered. Members of the Tonopah Lions Club, including Joe Friel and Roy Wolfe, helped establish the Beatty club, which met every Monday night in the basement of the Exchange Club for dinner and to plan charitable activities, including raising money to help poor people in the area receive eye care and eyeglasses (R. and C. Lisle, 1987; F. and E. Brockman, 1987).

Because Beatty lacked a chamber of commerce, the Lions Club also assumed typical chamber activities. Members of the club answered letters from individuals around the country who desired information on Beatty, and they worked closely with chambers of commerce in Tonopah and Las Vegas. Jack Crowell, the Lions Club's first president, remembered that the organization also served as a social club for the town. It helped community members meet each other and provided a basis for get-togethers (J. and M-K. Crowell, 1987).

Burro races, one of the Lions Club's most interesting activities during the 1960s and early 1970s, began in 1961 and lasted for twelve years. Contestants had to lead a recently captured wild burro over a pre-established course. Rules required the contestant to place a halter and pack on the critter, which demonstrated its displeasure by plenty of kicking and biting. The best athletes were able to control the burros most effectively; they could run fast, thus keeping the burro's mind off what was going on (J. and M-K. Crowell, 1987).

Burro races were held on Armistice Day and coincided with the forty-niners' annual celebration in Death Valley. It proved to be a very popular three-day affair—in fact, too popular. When the burro races became more widely known, the events began to attract rowdies from other areas and for too many people the affair became a three-day drunk. In 1972 the races were discontinued because many townspeople reluctantly concluded that the rowdies and drunks, who had come to dominate the affair, were bad for the community's image and safety, and their presence negated the event's benefits (J. and M-K. Crowell, 1987).

Tourism

Although Beatty began as a mining and railroad town, by the beginning of World War II rail service had ceased; by the end of World War II the era of the small miner had ended and mining was reduced to a supplementary role in the local economy. After the 1940s, tourism slowly emerged as one of two dominant features in the community's drive to survive and grow. (The other feature was the defense-related employment at Nellis and the Nevada Test Site.) Beatty was well positioned to capitalize on the postwar growth of tourism. It is located in the heart of the last great flowering of the Old West in America and is also one of the gateways to Death Valley, which was granted national monument status on February 11, 1933. The emergence of nearby (by Nevada standards) Las Vegas as a world-class tourist destination was an additional factor.

The growth of tourism in Beatty can be clearly seen for one period following World War II in figures from the old *Beatty Bulletin*. In 1944, 55 vehicles a day came from the north into Beatty. Between 1948 and 1949, traffic over Highway 95 increased substantially, with 206 vehicles a day coming from the north in 1949 compared to 109 the year before; more than half had out-of-state license plates. In 1949 an average of 48 cars a day came into town over Daylight Pass. In that same year, a total of 440 cars entered Beatty daily compared to 336 the year before ("Traffic Flow into Beatty Increases 40 Per Cent," 1949). In 1954, the annual encampment of the Death Valley Forty-Niners was expected to draw 10,000 people ("Death Valley Will Again Be Site of Exciting Activities," 1954).

It took a couple of decades for many people in Beatty to realize just how dependent the town had become on tourism. The severe flood of 1969 helped drive the point home. The problem began when Beatty and the upper reaches of the Amargosa drainage area were blanketed with 6 inches of wet snow, followed by a steady, warm rain. The rain and melting snow combined to send a torrent down the Amargosa River and Oasis Valley, inundating the lower sections of the community and washing out the bridge below the Beatty Narrows. The flood severed Highway 95 north and south of Beatty, cutting off all travel into the town for several days. With transportation cut, residents were immediately impressed by the extent to which the community had come to rely on tourist travel and its impact on stores, motels, and gas stations. They saw how vital travel over Daylight Pass to Death Valley was for many residents' livelihoods. They also realized the important role truck traffic played in the town's economy (J. and M-K. Crowell, 1987).

In recent years, recreational vehicles have further increased the importance of tourist travel in Beatty's economy. More and more older Americans have become nomadic. They live in campers or motor homes and travel about the country as they wish. In the 1980s, additional RV facilities were developed within Beatty and on its outskirts. Tourist travel in and out of Beatty tends to be heaviest from Washington's birthday until about Easter or Mother's Day. Motels are heavily booked during this period. Of particular importance during this season are the "snowbirds"—seminomadic citizens who leave the northern areas of the country during the winter season to take advantage of the warm weather in the Southwest. When the weather turns hot, the snowbirds migrate back north (J. and M-K. Crowell, 1987).

The Brockmans Construct a Motel

Frank and Edith Brockman moved to Beatty in 1957. Edith is the daughter of Gordon Bettles, who lived on the T&T Ranch in the Amargosa Valley from the late 1940s until the early 1960s. Gordon had encouraged Frank and Edith, who were living in Ridgecrest, California, to acquire land on the T&T Ranch; but a California agricultural agent advised them (wrongly it turned out) against it because of the presence of creosote brush, which he thought indicated the land would not be suitable for agriculture. However, after Edith suffered a severe leg injury in a serious automobile accident, the Brockmans decided to acquire property in Beatty and build a small motel.

Through the Brockmans' first efforts to purchase land in Beatty, they learned that the nature of business transactions in Nevada was very different than in California: A handshake in Beatty was worth more than a contract in California. People like Gordon Bettles, Ralph Lisle, Art Revert, and Warren Doing conducted business on the basis of verbal agreements and notes scribbled on paper. Even very large parcels of property were sold in this manner. Moreover, a person's word in Nevada might be more reliable than a formal contract elsewhere. Keeping one's word was a matter of honor, and an individual's honor sealed all deals (F. and E. Brockman, 1987).

However, when Brockman attempted to purchase property in Beatty, he found that handshakes were not reflected in county records and it was not always clear who was the legal owner of a particular piece of property. After some discussion, he purchased Block 80 from Warren Doing, owner of the Exchange Club, for the taxes Doing owed on it. When Brockman asked Doing why he was not making a profit, Doing answered that he had acquired the property for taxes and was selling it for taxes. Block 80, which consisted of twenty 50-x-100-foot lots, was located across Highway 95 at what was then the far south end of the community; only a corral and a small white house lay beyond the site (F. and E. Brockman, 1987).

Brockman then began construction of a five-unit motel, the Desert Inn. He obtained a bulldozer and began clearing and leveling the lot. At one time, the site had been part of the old locomotive service area—the "Y" where LV&T locomotives were turned around for the reverse run to Rhyolite. While excavating, Brockman uncovered an old tar pit about the size of a locomotive, where creosote from the locomotives' firebox had been scraped and allowed to accumulate. He filled the old tar pit with sand; the motel office was constructed over the old pit. It took Brockman approximately two years to build the motel. Its units became a home away from home for people working on the X-15 project and the radar facility, which was in operation between 1959 and 1968.

In true frontier fashion—and despite her severe leg injury—Edith worked alongside Frank to run and maintain the motel. She remembered ironing bedsheets on a mangle that had been converted to gas from electricity. Although the Brockmans remained in town only a few years, they were also involved in several community endeavors, including the establishment of an ambulance service in Beatty. Before the service was established, people had to be transported to the hospital in the sheriff department's station wagon; oil cans and tools were quickly removed from the wagon when it was needed. The Brockmans were also involved in the Lions Club, which coordinated drivers to create the ambulance service (F. and E. Brockman, 1987).

From Waitress to Blue-ribbon Businesswoman

Jane Cottonwood spent her early childhood in the eastern United States. Then her family moved to Los Angeles for several years, and Jane attended school there. In 1949 the family decided to move to the desert. They were unable to find a place to live in Las Vegas and moved to Beatty. While attending school in Tonopah, Jane met Ted "Bombo" Cottonwood and later they were married. In 1951 the newlyweds returned to live in Beatty, where Bombo had grown up (J. Cottonwood, 1987). For many years Jane worked long hours as a waitress at the Exchange Club and across the street at the Wagonwheel Restaurant.

The Cottonwoods had two daughters who became 4-H members when they were older; Jane became a 4-H leader. She was pleased when the girls became interested in horses. They loved to participate in horse shows, especially gymkhana, which involved games on horseback such as barrel races. At first, the girls' participation in gymkhana took them to small horse shows at Indian Springs and other small neighboring communities, but as the girls' skills improved they found themselves in Las Vegas and Reno. Soon Jane was putting on a horse show in Beatty each year during the first week of May (J. Cottonwood, 1987).

Hosting horse shows opened a new world for Jane. Winners of contests were awarded ribbons and trophies, which Jane had to purchase. In the mid-1960s, although there were two trophy and ribbon shops in Las Vegas, orders had to be placed months in advance because the Las Vegas stores had to get their ribbons and trophies from manufacturers in Texas and Ohio. One day when she was discussing the difficulty of obtaining ribbons with the owner of Trophies of Las Vegas, Jane commented, "I don't think it's such a big thing; anybody can make those ribbons."

"Gee," the owner replied, "I wish you could." This conversation started Jane thinking. Perhaps she could make her own ribbons. It might even be possible to supplement the family income in this way. She took some ribbons apart on her kitchen table to see how they were made and confirmed her suspicion that they would be easy to manufacture. She thought about this project off and on for a couple of years (J. Cottonwood, 1987).

One day in 1967, she mentioned the idea to a friend who was an accountant. He was impressed and offered to invest $4000 to start Jane in the ribbon-making business. Thus began Janda Ribbons—a business venture that is a dream come true for Jane Cottonwood as well as an American success story (J. Cottonwood, 1987).

In her small house in Beatty, Jane began making the ribbons in the living room and printing letters on them in the master bedroom. She sold her first orders to Trophies of Las Vegas and soon obtained a contract from people who were putting on a fair in California. The living room and bedroom became cluttered with ribbon production, and Bombo offered to build her a "factory." He constructed a 16-x-20-foot building next door to the house and, as Jane said, "He has never quit building to this day." Since the construction of the first garage-sized building, Jane Cottonwood's ribbon factory has grown room by room. The 16-x-20-foot addition that Bombo originally constructed did not suffice for long. He soon built a 16-x-30-foot addition and then added a 10-x-50-foot trailer for the manufacture of trophies. When the operation outgrew the trailer, he added a 24-x-55-foot building. At that point the Cottonwoods moved out of their home and built a new one; the business now occupied their old home. Thus, the manufacturing facility grew by modules, with each module constructed by Bombo (J. Cottonwood, 1987).

Soon after she started the business, Jane found she had to hire help; and the more she hired, the more it seemed she needed. Demand for Janda Ribbons became so great that it was unnecessary to put any effort into selling. Customers were impressed with the price and quality and would seek Jane out. She never had to advertise; word of mouth was sufficient. (For many years Janda Ribbons was not even listed in the phone directory.) Jane added trophies and, later, plaques to her product line. In recent years, she added items for sale in gift shops and awards fashioned of silver (J. Cottonwood, 1987).

High demand for Jane's product necessitated a constant search, one that continues today, for suppliers of materials and for machines that can speed up and automate the manufacturing processes. Much of the search is trial and error. Because Beatty is geographically isolated, Jane buys two of every mechanical device so she will have a backup for anything that breaks down. In addition to continuously constructing new facilities, Bombo repairs all the machines (J. Cottonwood, 1987).

For several years, Janda Ribbons has been a major employer in Beatty. There were 30 employees in the summer of 1991, with 24 to 26 working during the off-season. The number of peak-season employees is down slightly from a few years ago because of increased automation. Jane is proud that most of her employees are highly skilled and have been with her for years. The turnover at the ribbon factory is low, with only one new employee added in 1991. Local high school students are hired during the summer, the peak season for business. Most of the employees are women who live in Beatty or the nearby Amargosa Valley.

Because of Beatty's isolation, shipping and receiving was a problem for many years. About ten years ago United Parcel Service (UPS) began delivery to Beatty, which has considerably relieved the problem. Janda Ribbons can now place an order with a supplier on the East Coast and receive the product through UPS the next day; shipping has also been expedited. With its high volume, the ribbon factory is a major Beatty client for UPS. Though Jane likes to keep a low profile, the business is so successful that it has become a local tourist attraction. Bus tours of the area regularly visit the Janda factory.

For many years, most of Janda Ribbons' clients were in the western United States—California, Nevada, Arizona, Montana, Texas, and Oklahoma, but now Jane does business throughout the country and has even expanded into New Zealand. Managers of fairs and other potential customers are almost always willing to see her. She makes calls in the off-season between October and the first of April. Once people see her prices and quality, she usually gets the sale (J. Cottonwood, 1987).

Asked the secret of her success, Jane replied that she always has had a lot of energy; she worked hard as a waitress and is working just as hard, if not harder, now. Price and product quality are vital to her business achievements, and she is optimistic about future growth (J. Cottonwood, 1987).

A Radar Project

In about 1958, the federal government constructed a radar facility north of Beatty, about 2-1/2 miles north of Springdale to the west of Highway 95. The Beatty radar site was perched on a mountain and offered a good view of Sarcobatus Flat to the north. The facility monitored, by radar and radio communications, flight tests of experimental aircraft operating out of Edwards Air Force Base, located on the desert northeast of Los Angeles. At first, personnel were flown from Edwards Air Force Base to the site when flight tests were to be conducted and then flown out when tests were over. When this proved to be both expensive and disruptive to staffing at Edwards, a permanent staff of about 10 was placed at the Beatty facility from 1959 to 1968. The members of the staff and their families lived in Beatty.

During that period, William J. "Bill" Houck was the site manager and coordinator between NASA (the agency conducting the tests) and a series of three private contractors who, over the years, had successfully bid on the job of running the radar facility: initially the Bendix Corporation, then Unitech, followed by RCA. During flight tests, the facility electronically monitored activities with radar, telemetry, and voice communication. Among the aircraft monitored were the F-104, F-107, B-70, SR-71 (Blackbird), X-15, and X-24.

Tests of the X-15 were among the most important and best remembered by local residents. The X-15 was a high-flying, experimental aircraft that was air-launched from a B-52 at about 45,000 feet elevation; powered by rocket engines, it soared to heights in excess of 350,000 feet, at speeds of more than 4,000 miles per hour. At such speeds and elevations, it was, in effect, a suborbital spacecraft and its pilots were really astronauts. The X-15 was launched in northern Nevada not far from Wendover, Utah, and, if everything went as planned, landed at Edwards Air Force Base. Designated emergency landing sites included Mud Lake south of Tonopah—which was used a couple of times—and Sarcobatus Flat north of Beatty, which was never used. During flight, the X-15 was continuously electronically tracked by a succession of radar facilities at Ely, Beatty, and Edwards. The facility at Ely was very similar to the one at Beatty.

Electric power for the site was obtained from on-site generators during the first years of operation, but hooked into Hoover Dam power when it became available in Beatty through the Valley Electric Association. During tests, backup generators were always running in case of a power failure, however.

Neil Armstrong, the first man to walk on the moon, was one of the test pilots in the X-15 program. After the radar station was closed in 1968, the facility was dismantled and title to the site reverted to the U.S. Bureau of Land Management. The facility at Ely was operated for 2-1/2 years after the closure of the one at Beatty.

A Low-Level Radioactive Waste Storage Facility

A low-level radioactive waste disposal facility, operated by U.S. Ecology, is located several miles south of Beatty near Highway 95. The facility, which began operating in the early 1960s, provides a steady source of employment for a dozen or so families in the area and further strengthens the community's pioneering role in the development of nuclear technology.

Beatty residents regret that the facility has become something of a political football in recent years. As with the Nevada Test Site, few people in the community complain about the site or its method of operation. Most believe that the operators of the facility have been good neighbors. U.S. Ecology has made numerous donations to community projects, including the fund for fire trucks and an annual scholarship to a graduating senior from Beatty High School. Moreover, the company often lends its heavy equipment when the community needs it (for example, a cherry-picker crane was needed to raise and decorate the community Christmas tree and a grader was needed in the construction of the ballpark).

People in Beatty view with concern the critical public and media portrayal of nuclear research and nuclear waste disposal, and they are amused by the media's occasional portrayal of them as people who are careless with radioactive tools and equipment obtained from the disposal facility. Most are quick to point out a phenomenon long observed by sociologists—namely, the farther away one gets from something disliked or feared, the more ominous and dangerous it is perceived to be. In reference to the Test Site and the possibility of a high-level radioactive waste repository at nearby Yucca Mountain, a resident said,

> The closer you live to it, the less people are opposed to it, it seems. Someone could say we're a bunch of dummies. But that's not the case. We in this area have had more experience with the safe use of nuclear technology than practically any place in the world. Certainly, if there were going to be harm, you would see it here. But you don't; we're healthy and happy as a bunch of coyotes (J. and M-K. Crowell, 1987).

The Proposed Yucca Mountain Repository

Since the U.S. Congress passed the Nuclear Waste Policy Act in 1982, there has been a great deal of activity by the U.S. Department of Energy to determine the geotechnical suitability of Yucca Mountain to be the nation's first high-level nuclear waste geologic repository. Yucca Mountain is located approximately 15 miles southeast of Beatty, Nevada, on land controlled by the federal government. The facility must be designed to safely isolate large quantities of highly toxic and dangerous nuclear waste from the human environment for 10,000 years, and the DOE will not know if the location is suitable until site characterization is completed around the year 2000 (Bradhurst, 1991).

If the site is judged to be geotechnically suitable, the DOE must then receive a permit to construct and operate the proposed nuclear waste repository from the Nuclear Regulatory Commission. Under even the most optimistic scenarios, it is not expected that a repository would be operational until the end of the first decade of the twenty-first century (Bradhurst, 1991).

Late in December 1987, the U.S. Congress passed legislation that amended the 1982 Nuclear Waste Policy Act in order to single out Yucca Mountain as the prime candidate site for storage of high-level nuclear waste. Supporters of the 1987 amendment feel that the government's singling out Yucca Mountain for the possible storage of high-level nuclear waste is proper given the area's aridity and sparse population, the large amount of nuclear testing that has taken place at the Nevada Test Site over more than 35 years, and the necessity of restricting the area for thousands of years to come regardless of future waste storage projects.

Those opposed to a nuclear waste repository at Yucca Mountain point out that there is a big difference between the relatively small levels of waste produced through nuclear testing and the large amounts planned for storage. They argue that most nuclear waste is produced in the eastern United States and that Nevada has done enough for the country with the atomic testing program and its many military installations. Moreover, they fear the unknown problems such a facility might present (Bradhurst, 1991).

Employment Woes

Throughout most of Beatty's history, employment has been the major problem; usually there have not been enough job opportunities. Since the 1950s a major employer has been the Nevada Test Site. Those who have jobs there either live part-time in worker housing on the facility and return home on weekends or else make a long commute each day. Some live in Mercury (although no families can reside there)—

a federally owned, restricted-access community located on the Test Site. Mercury, named after an old mine in the area, serves as an on-site headquarters and primary staging area for Nevada Test Site operations. It is located just off Highway 95, about 60 miles northeast of Las Vegas and 55 miles from Beatty. Some workers must drive another 30 to 40 miles to their jobs on the Test Site, which adds up to as much as 200 miles of travel daily. (Previously, Beatty residents could enter the Test Site through the shortcut near Lathrop Wells. However, this route has been closed for some time [J. and M-K. Crowell, 1987].)

Many Beatty residents are concerned and disgruntled that Test Site contractors hire workers out of union halls in Las Vegas rather than also making an effort to work through local channels. Because the Test Site is in their backyard, residents have long asked for a hiring outlet in Beatty; but these requests have never produced results.

It is also evident that DOE has not made an effort to employ Beatty residents on its Yucca Mountain project. Between 1983 and the end of fiscal year 1991, the U.S. Department of Energy spent in excess of $850 million in preliminary efforts to determine Yucca Mountain's suitability; yet this expenditure has produced no more than two jobs in Beatty on repository-related activity and none in the Amargosa Valley—the other community that is close to Yucca Mountain (Bradhurst, 1991; U.S. Department of Energy, 1991). Residents are hopeful that if federal plans for a high-level nuclear waste repository at nearby Yucca Mountain materialize, local workers will be given job opportunities. Many believe that a type of affirmative action for hiring should be practiced, with locals given preference over residents from other areas, both at the Test Site and other nearby government projects.

Federal Rules

Many Beatty residents felt the pinch of new federal and state regulations during the 1970s and 1980s. The federal government's insistence that drivers hold to a 55-mph speed limit on Nevada's high-quality rural highways, such as Highway 95, is very unpopular, as are the state's efforts to enforce this law. Many long for a return of the day when there was no speed limit and Highway 95 in Nye County was not patrolled. Most people feel that speed limits appropriate in New Jersey or Rhode Island are not appropriate for rural Nevada.

Federal mining laws, however well intended, can make problems for local mine operators. For instance, these laws specify that mining operators can only hire a worker who has received 40 hours of training. Although this requirement seems reasonable, for small mining operations such as the Crowell Mine, it means that an inexperienced person cannot legally be hired unless given a full week of training. Prior to this training, the mine operator has no knowledge of how the new employee will work out. The employee might not be a good worker and might not even wish to work in the mine after receiving the training. Crowell and others believe young miners are best integrated into the mine work force gradually, beginning with simple tasks and the slowly increasing the skill level. If a new worker does not like the work and quits, an unwarranted economic burden is not placed on the mine operator. Local operators note that the government advises the operator to pass the expense of training on to the customers. That may be possible, one said cynically, "if your competitors aren't in Mexico" (J. and M-K. Crowell, 1987).

The prohibition of mining activity within the boundaries of the Death Valley National Monument eliminated small-scale operations. During the 1930s, there were a number of old prospectors working small claims in the Panamint, Funeral, and Grapevine mountains on either side of Death Valley. The mining operations were very small, one-man affairs, confined to the use of hand tools following narrow, but sometimes very rich, veins of gold. The veins were known for their spotty occurrence. The miners were also sometimes working small placers. Ralph Lisle recalls how the old-timers would bring their small caches of nuggets and dust into Charlie Brown's store in Shoshone, California, and sell or trade them for supplies. Lisle and others believe that such small, low-impact mining operations are a part of the area's colorful past and should be allowed to continue. Such operations, they believe, could be conducted with minimal impact on the environment and would boost the local economy by providing opportunities for self-employment (R. Lisle, 1989).

Supporters of the prohibition on mining would argue, however, that the total integrity of all park land should be protected. They believe that exceptions should not be made for short-term gains.

A Caring Town

Although Beatty is a small community not known for its wealth, it has the reputation, of which the residents are very proud, of being a caring town. As Chloe Lisle said, "over the years many people have put themselves back into the town." Bert Lemmon agreed: "I have seen here in town, periods where you could shoot a cannonball down Main Street and you wouldn't hit anything but a sleeping dog. You wouldn't think there was a hundred dollars in the town. But [if somebody has] a tragic accident, see how quick, within an hour, there's a thousand dollars or so which has been raised. Yes, I've seen it happen many a time" (R. and C. Lisle, 1987).

Bombo Cottonwood reinforced this picture with recollec-
tions of his childhood in the late 1930s and 1940s:

> There was always somebody buying anything that you
> [the youngsters] could scrape up [such as arrowheads, etc.].
> They were taking care of us kids, more than anything.
> Instead of just giving us money, they'd make us work for it.
> That's the way the old sheriff [Vignolo] used to be: If he
> didn't have anything for me to do, he'd just hand me a nickel.
> And, boy, whenever he needed something done [such as
> weeding or cleaning out his chicken coop], I'd better do
> it.... No, they all looked after us kids (T. Cottonwood, 1987).

Another facet of community caring is demonstrated by
residents' keen alertness to the sound of a siren; to them, the
siren means someone needs help, such as medical assistance
or fighting a fire. When visiting a big city, such as Las Vegas,
they find themselves instinctively responding. As Maud-
Kathrin Crowell said, "Well, you can tell we're hicks, because
what do we do? We're straining our eyes to see what's going
on, because here in Beatty a siren means to come and help. In
Las Vegas it means get out of the way." Jack Crowell added,
"In Las Vegas each person thinks somebody else is going to do
it, because in the cities somebody else does do it. In the rural
area, it's different. If the individual himself doesn't render aid,
it may not get done!" (J. and M-K. Crowell, 1987).

CHAPTER 8

The Future

eatty residents feel that the community has been fortunate over the years in having been spared the boom-and-bust economy that has character-ized so many other communities in the rural West. They point out that even during the Rhyolite boom Beatty remained relatively small; Rhyolite's collapse left Beatty to survive and grow on its own. Over the years growth was slow and sporadic.

Yet in 1930 Shorty Harris prophetically noted:

> There was plenty of gold in those mountains when I discovered the original Bullfrog, and there's plenty there yet. . . . Stock speculation—that's what killed Rhyolite! The promotors got impatient. They figured that money could be made faster by getting gold from the pockets of suckers than by digging it out of the hills (Harris, 1930: 20).

Then Harris made a prediction: "If the right people ever get hold of Rhyolite they'll make a killing; but they'll have to be real hard-rock miners, and not the kind that do their work only on paper" (Harris, 1930:20).

Shorty Harris had no way of knowing that it would take advances in technology to make his prediction come true, but true it proved to be, nevertheless. Advances in gold and silver refining and extraction chemistry involving the use of a weak cyanide solution in "heap leaching" in the late 1960s and early 1970s enabled modern miners to economically operate on gold and silver ores that run as little as .02 of an ounce of gold per ton—that involves processing 50 tons of rock to obtain 1 ounce of gold (Potts, 1989). (Twenty-five tons of unbroken rock will cover a 17-foot-square living room floor about 2 foot deep.) Such developments in refining technology meant that gold miners no longer had to restrict themselves to narrow seams of ore that meandered through rock formations beneath the earth's surface, first appearing and then disappearing unpredictably. Miners no longer had to engage in the expensive and dangerous labor of drilling, blasting, mucking, tramming, hoisting to the surface, sorting, and milling only the most select portions of a gold-bearing block of ground. With heap leaching, large portions of a geological formation— in some cases an entire mountain—could be blasted, hauled to crushers on trucks large enough to carry a locomotive, then placed on leaching pads where a weak cyanide solution circulated over the crushed rock leaches out the gold and silver. By the late 1980s, heap-leaching technology had transformed the gold mining industry in Nevada: the state produced more than half the nation's and 5 percent of the world's gold (Dye, 1989:1BB). Much of the latter-day gold boom in Nevada was centered on old mining camps, where entire mountains into which old-time miners had once tunneled were being removed and processed, including Round Mountain in northern Nye County.

Several large deposits of minable gold and silver ores have been found in the Beatty area, and a number of large open-pit mines are either operating or undergoing construction. The largest of these is the Bond Gold Bullfrog Mine. In 1983, St. Joe American, an exploration arm of St. Joe Minerals Corporation, purchased the Montgomery Shoshone property for $49,500 from Robert Revert, who had bought it in the 1950s for taxes. The company began drilling the site, expecting to locate 10 million tons of workable ore, averaging 0.05 ounces of gold per ton. By 1983, only 5 million tons had been delineated—an insufficient amount necessary to yield an adequate profit on the required invested capital.

Additional analysis of the fault structure of the district, however, revealed conditions on the east side of Ladd Mountain that were similar to those around the Montgomery Shoshone Mine and the original Bullfrog Mine. Further drilling in 1986 and 1987 on the east side of Ladd Mountain—not far from where Senator Stewart once hoped to find gold—led to the discovery of an underground orebody estimated to contain 16.4 million tons of mill-grade ore averaging 0.105 ounces of gold (for an estimated total of 1,547,000 ounces of gold) and trace amounts of silver. Aptly illustrating the miner's lament, "so close, but so far," the 1986 drill hole on Ladd Mountain, which first produced an excellent intercept of the orebody, was located near an old shaft that had missed the ore zone by only 35 feet (Hall, 1989:8–14). It is doubtful that turn-of-the-century mining technology could have operated at a profit on such low-grade ore, though there might have been streaks of richer values in the orebody that could have been successfully mined. But imagine the promotional potential for such a find during Rhyolite's boom period. Moreover, it has been reported that activities on Ladd Mountain during this period uncovered at least one gold-bearing vein containing up to 6 ounces of gold per ton within a few feet of the surface. Such discoveries, no doubt, have made many old Rhyolite miners and promoters turn over in their graves.

With an economic orebody clearly defined, in late 1987 work got under way. First, a feasibility study and operational plan were undertaken. Working with local, state, and federal officials, company representatives designed an operation so as not to adversely impact the area's cultural resources, including nearby Shoshone rock shelters and a chert quarry; Rhyolite and Bullfrog cemeteries and trash dumps; remnants of Rhyolite's water system, power lines and poles, and railroads; wildlife, including reptiles, songbirds, and wild burros; and the area's groundwater. A water supply for mine operation was secured, equipment moved in, an ore-crushing and milling system installed, and a gold recovery plant constructed. During the peak of the construction phase, a total of 540 workers were employed. To help accommodate the sudden influx of workers, additional mobile home parks were created in Beatty, along with a temporary camp housing 300 people. The first bar of gold from the new Bullfrog Mine was poured July 25, 1989. In August 1989, the permanent workforce totaled 320 (Hall, 1989:12–19).

The initial drilling of the orebody was carried out by St. Joe American company, but in 1987, Australian entrepreneur Alan Bond, through his Dallhold Resources Inc., paid $500 million for St. Joe's gold properties. Dallhold Resources later became Bond International Gold, Inc. In 1989 LAC Minerals Ltd., based in Toronto, Canada, purchased the 65 percent controlled by Alan Bond; LAC currently (1991) operates the mine. It is expected that the mine will produce about 240,000 ounces of gold per year during its life, and hopes run high for additional future discoveries in the area (Hall, 1989:11–20).

Beatty's population with the latest mining boom increased from about 1000 in 1980 to between 1500 and 2000 at the end of 1990; if no new mines are brought into production, the population is expected to level off at about 2800 through 1995, then fall again after the turn of the century (Planning Information Corporation, 1988:i). Thus, 80 years after the balloon burst at Rhyolite, Beatty, like so many of its sister communities in rural Nevada, is caught in a boom-and-bust cycle. If the federal government decides to go ahead with development of a high-level nuclear waste repository at nearby Yucca Mountain, activities could pick up the slack caused by reduced mining.

Yet, despite recent growth, the people of Beatty consider their community a fine place in which to live. Most believe that they are fortunate to have lived free from so many of the problems that characterize larger communities. They know firsthand the benefits of life in rural Nevada. As one long-time Beatty resident put it, "We who have lived out in the country like our freedom" (C. Lisle, 1991). Residents of Beatty value a lifestyle still close to the frontier and cherish the values of honesty, personal freedom, respect for the individual, optimism about the future, and a basic "can-do" attitude. They are determined to preserve their present high quality of life (J. and M-K. Crowell, 1987).

References

"AEC Issues Warnings as Atomic Tests Near." *Beatty Bulletin*. March 6, 1953.

"AEC Moves to Protect Persons in this Area." *Beatty Bulletin*. March 13, 1953.

"Air Force Seeks to Buy Rights on Bomb Range." *Beatty Bulletin*. July 24, 1953.

"Atomic Damage Claims Decline." *Beatty Bulletin*. March 27, 1953.

"Atomic Explosions Are Unpredictable, Writes Witness of Two Blasts." *Beatty Bulletin*. January 19, 1951.

"Bates Family Purchases Spacious Bullfrog Motel." *Beatty Bulletin*. October 1, 1948.

"Beatty Appears to Be Nearest Town to Site of Atomic Tests." *Beatty Bulletin*. January 19, 1951.

Beatty Bulletin. Supplement to the *Goldfield News*. April 25, 1947–December 28, 1956. Referenced in this document by article heading.

"Beatty Mourns Passing of Beloved Dad Revert." *Beatty Bulletin*. May 15, 1953.

"Beatty Shows Population Growth in Past Decade." *Beatty Bulletin*. July 7, 1950.

"Beatty Supports Its Candidates." *Beatty Bulletin*. November 5, 1948.

"Beatty to Have Catholic Church." *Beatty Bulletin*. February 24, 1956.

Bradhurst, Stephen T. Personal communication. 1991.

Brockman, Frank and Edith. *An Interview with Frank and Edith Brockman.* Nye County Town History Project, Tonopah, NV. 1987.

Brooks, Thomas W. *By Buckboard to Beatty. The California-Nevada Desert in 1886.* Edited, with introduction and notes by Anthony L. Lehman. Los Angeles: Dawson's Book Shop. 1970.

"Bullfrog to Add Seven New Units." *Beatty Bulletin.* May 23, 1947.

Carlson, Helen S. *Nevada Places Names: A Geographical Dictionary.* Reno: University of Nevada Press. 1974.

Caruthers, William. *Loafing Along the Death Valley Trails: A Personal Narrative of People and Places.* Ontario, CA: Death Valley Publishing Co. 1951.

Charney, Jean. Personal communication. 1987.

Cline, Gloria Griffen, *Peter Skene Odgen and the Hudson's Bay Company.* Norman: University of Oklahoma Press. 1974.

"Construction of 12-Unit Motel Launched by Epps." *Beatty Bulletin.* August 27, 1948.

"Continue Efforts to Secure 'Night' Phone for Beatty." *Beatty Bulletin.* December 10, 1948.

Cottonwood, Jane. *An Interview with Jane Cottonwood.* Nye County Town History Project, Tonopah, NV. 1987.

Cottonwood, Ted "Bombo." *An Interview with Ted "Bombo" Cottonwood.* Nye County Town History Project, Tonopah, NV. 1987.

Crowell, Jack. Personal communication. 1991.

Crowell, Jack, and Maud-Kathrin. *An Interview with Jack and Maud-Kathrin Crowell.* Nye County Town History Project, Tonopah, NV. 1987.

———. Personal communication. 1989.

Crowell, J. Irving, and Dorothy. *An Interview with Irving and Dorothy Crowell.* Nye County Town History Project, Tonopah, NV. 1987.

Davies, Grace. *An Interview with Grace Davies.* Nye County Town History Project, Tonopah, NV. 1987.

D'Azevedo, Warren L., ed. *Great Basin.* Vol. 11 of *Handbook of North American Indians.* Washington, DC: Smithsonian Institution. 1986.

"Death Valley Will Again Be Site of Exciting Activities." *Beatty Bulletin*. November 5, 1954.

"Disclose Sale of Gateway Trailer Park to Porter." *Beatty Bulletin*. February 20, 1948.

"District Loses True Friend in Death of A. M. Johnson." *Beatty Bulletin*. January 16, 1948.

"District Voting Power Shows Increase of 39 Per Cent." *Beatty Bulletin*. October 22, 1948.

Dye, Tom. "Gold Rush Heading Toward Las Vegas." *Las Vegas Review-Journal*. March 19, 1989.

"East Coast Columnist Terms Beatty Livelier than LA and Hollywood." *Beatty Bulletin*. July 21, 1950.

Egan, Ferol. *Fremont, Explorer for a Restless Nation*. Garden City, NY: Doubleday. 1977. Reprinted by University of Nevada Press, Reno. 1985.

Elliott, Russell R. *Nevada's Twentieth-Century Mining Boom: Tonopah, Goldfield, Ely*. Reno: University of Nevada Press. 1966.

————. *History of Nevada*. Lincoln: University of Nebraska Press. 1984.

"Few See Flash from Big Burst." *Beatty Bulletin*. April 10, 1953.

"Fire Station Building to Be Moved to Beatty." *Beatty Bulletin*. September 16, 1949.

"Fire Truck Can't Reach Site of Blaze." *Beatty Bulletin*. December 5, 1947.

"Flames Destroy Lisle Garage, Gas Station." *Beatty Bulletin*. December 25, 1953.

Gillette, Dolores "Dolly." *An Interview with Dolores "Dolly" Gillette*. Nye County Town History Project, Tonopah, NV. 1987.

————. Personal communication. 1989.

Gower, Harry P. *50 Years in Death Valley—Memoirs of a Borax Man*. Introduction by James M. Gerstley. Published by the Death Valley '49ers. Publication No. 9. San Bernardino, CA: Inland Printing and Engraving Company. 1969.

Hall, Robin G. *Bullfrog District: A Second Boom*. Denver: Bond Gold Corporation. 1989.

Hanes, Richard C. "Cultural Persistence in Nevada: Current Native American Issues." *Journal of California and Great Basin Anthropology*. Vol. 4, No. 2, pp. 203–221. 1982.

Harris, Frank "Shorty." "Half a Century Chasing Rainbows." *Westways*, pp. 12–20. October 1930.

Houck, William J. Personal communication. 1991.

Hulse, James W. *The Nevada Adventure: A History*. Reno: University of Nevada Press. First published, 1965; fifth edition, 1981.

"Ike Shaw Burned Fatally in Blaze." *Beatty Bulletin*. February 5, 1954.

"Influx of New Families Taxes Beatty's Housing." *Beatty Bulletin*. August 17, 1951.

Johnson, Leroy, and Jean. *Escape from Death Valley*. Reno: University of Nevada Press. 1987.

Kerr, John. "Beatty's Projects Good as Gold." *Las Vegas Review-Journal*. March 19, 1989.

Latschar, John A. *Historic Resource Study: A History of Mining in Death Valley National Monument*. Vol. II. Denver, CO: National Park Service. 1981.

Lee, Bourke. *Death Valley Men*. New York: Macmillan. 1932.

Lincoln, Francis Church. *Mining Districts and Mineral Resources of Nevada*. Reno: Nevada Newsletter Publishing Co. 1923. Reprinted by Nevada Publications, Las Vegas. 1982.

Lingenfelter, Richard E. *The Hardrock Miners*. Berkeley: University of California Press. 1974.

———. *Death Valley and the Amargosa: A Land of Illusion*. Berkeley: University of California Press. 1986.

Lingenfelter, Richard E., and Karen Rix Gash. *The Newspapers of Nevada: A History and Bibliography, 1854–1979*. Reno: University of Nevada Press. 1984.

Lisle, Chloe C. Personal communication. 1989.

———. Personal communication. 1991.

Lisle, Ralph F. Personal communication. 1989.

———. Personal communication. 1991.

Lisle, Ralph F., and Chloe C. *An Interview with Ralph F. and Chloe C. Lisle.* Nye County Town History Project, Tonopah, NV. 1987.

McCracken, Robert D. *History Reports and Literature Reviews: Nye County, Amargosa Valley, Beatty, and Pahrump, Nevada.* SAIC, 101 Convention Center Drive, Las Vegas, NV 89109. 1986.

"Mill Tests to Start Next Week." *Beatty Bulletin.* July 16, 1948.

Moore, Ert A. *Experiences of a Pioneer Educator.* Reno, NV: Reno Oral History Project. 1979.

Myrick, David F. *Railroads of Nevada and Eastern California.* 2 vols. Berkeley, CA: Howell-North Books. Vol. 1, 1962; Vol. 2, 1963.

Neighbors, Roy. Personal communication. 1988.

"New Atom Jolt Brewing!" *Goldfield News.* October 5, 1951.

"New Beatty Trailer Park Composite of 'The Best.'" *Beatty Bulletin.* April 25, 1947.

"New Unit to Up Power Capacity by 50 Per Cent." *Beatty Bulletin.* November 28, 1947.

Noren, Evelyn. "John Fremont Dared What Others Dreamed." *Las Vegas Review-Journal,* "Nevadan," pp. 6L–7L. December 12, 1982.

Paher, Stanley W. *Las Vegas: As it Began—As It Grew.* Las Vegas: Nevada Publications. 1971.

Palmer, T. S., ed. *Place Names of the Death Valley Region in California and Nevada.* Originally published in 1948. Morongo Valley, CA: Sagebrush Press. 1980.

Planning Information Corporation. "Community Development Report: Town of Beatty, Nevada." Prepared for Nye County Board of Commissioners by Planning Information Corp., Denver, CO. August 1988.

Potts, Donald B. Personal communication. 1989.

"Quinn Plans Pilot Mill to Test Ore." *Beatty Bulletin.* November 28, 1947.

"Radar Site for Beatty." *Beatty Bulletin.* September 7, 1956.

Rafferty, Kevin, and Lynda Blair. *Billy Goat Peak: An Investigation and Reinterpretation of Virgin Anasazi and Paiute Prehistory and Ethnohistory.* DAS Report 2-5-9. Las Vegas: University of Nevada, Environmental Research Center. March 1984.

Ransome, F. L. *Mines of Goldfield, Bullfrog, and Other Southern Nevada Districts.* With notes on the Manhattan District by Garrey and Emmons. U.S. Geological Survey Bulletin 303 (originally titled *Preliminary Account of Goldfield, Bullfrog, and Other Mining Districts of Southern Nevada.* 1907). Republished by Nevada Publications, Las Vegas. 1983.

Records, Henry H. "Hank." *An Interview with Henry H. "Hank" Records.* Nye County Town History Project, Tonopah, NV. 1987.

Reidhead, Boyd, and Claudia. Personal communication. 1987.

Revert, Arthur. *An Interview with Arthur Revert.* Nye County Town History Project, Tonopah, NV. 1987.

Revert, Robert A. *An Interview with Robert A. Revert.* Nye County Town History Project, Tonopah, NV. 1988.

"Reynolds Concern Gets Proving Ground Pact." *Beatty Bulletin.* December 19, 1952.

Ritter, Betsy. *Life in the Ghost City of Rhyolite, Nevada.* Terra Bella, CA: Terra Bella News. 1939. Reprinted by Sagebrush Press, Morongo Valley, CA. 1982.

Rocha, Guy Louis, "Rhyolite: 1905–1940: An Historical Overview." In *Nye County History Project Historic Property Survey.* Tempe, AZ: Janus & Assoc., Inc. 1980.

Roske, Ralph J. *Las Vegas: A Desert Paradise.* Tulsa, OK: Continental Heritage Press. 1986.

"Scotty Buried on Hill Near Famed Castle." *Beatty Bulletin.* January 8, 1954.

"Secret Gold Hoard Hidden at Castle?" *Beatty Bulletin.* May 21, 1948.

"Sensation of the Mining World." *Bullfrog Miner.* May 12, 1906.

"Signs of Greater Prosperity Seen." *Beatty Bulletin.* June 6, 1947.

"'Small' Nuclear Tests in Store." *Beatty Bulletin.* October 14, 1955.

Spears, John R. *Illustrated Sketches of Death Valley and Other Borax Deserts of the Pacific Coast.* Chicago and New York: Rand, McNally & Co. 1892. Reissued by Sagebrush Press, Morongo Valley, CA. 1977.

"Speculation Rife on Exact Location of Nuclear Tests." *Beatty Bulletin.* January 19, 1951.

Sternberg, Sherry, Untitled manuscript on the history of the Valley Electric Association, later published in five segments. *Ruralite*. Forest Grove, OR: Ruralite Services, Inc. May–September 1986.

Steward, Julian H. *Basin-Plateau Aboriginal Sociopolitical Groups*. Washington, DC: Smithsonian Institution, Bureau of American Ethnology, Bulletin 120. 1938. Reprinted by University of Utah Press, Salt Lake City. 1970.

Stewart, Dan. *An Interview with Dan Stewart*. Lincoln County Town History Project, Pioche, NV. 1991.

"Survey May Presage Air Base Reactivation." *Beatty Bulletin*. October 5, 1951.

Terrell, Solan. *An Interview with Solan Terrell*. Nye County Town History Project, Tonopah, NV. 1987.

———. Personal communication. 1988.

Thomas, David Hurst. "An Overview of Central Great Basin Prehistory." In *Man and Environment in the Great Basin*, David B. Madsen and James F. O'Connell, eds., pp. 156–171. Washington, DC: The Society for American Archaeology. 1982.

Thomas, David Hurst, Lorann S. A. Pendleton, and Stephen C. Cappannari. "Western Shoshoni." In *Great Basin*, Warren L. D'Azevedo, ed. *Handbook of North American Indians*, Vol. 11, pp. 262–283. Washington, DC: Smithsonian Institution. 1986.

Titus, A. Costandina. *Bombs in the Backyard: Atomic Testing and American Politics*. Reno: University of Nevada Press. 1986.

"To Build 'Typical' City Near Here for A-Tests." *Beatty Bulletin*. December 5, 1952.

"To Conduct Atomic Tests Near Here." *Beatty Bulletin*. January 12, 1951.

"To Employ 1300 at Atomic Test Site." *Beatty Bulletin*. July 27, 1951.

"To Resume Atomic Tests Near Beatty." *Beatty Bulletin*. January 30, 1953.

"Traffic Flow into Beatty Increases 40 Per Cent." *Beatty Bulletin*. November 4, 1949.

"$2000 Annual Scholarship Established by Delfs' Will." *Beatty Bulletin*. May 4, 1956.

U.S. Department of Energy (Las Vegas office). Personal communication. 1991.

Weeks, James C. *An Interview with James C. Weeks.* Nye County Town History Project, Tonopah, NV. 1987.

Weight, Harold, and Lucile. *Rhyolite, The Ghost City of Golden Dreams.* Twentynine Palms, CA: Calico Press. 1972.

Wiley, Roland. Personal communication. 1991.

Wolkomir, Richard. "New Finds Could Rewrite the Start of American History." *Smithsonian*, Vol. 21, No. 12, pp. 130–144. March 1991.

"Yesterday's Atomic Jolt Clearly Seen, Heard, Felt Here." *Beatty Bulletin.* April 23, 1952.

Zanjani, Sally. "Jack Longstreet in the Death Valley Region." Paper presented at the Death Valley conference on Death Valley History, Furnace Creek, CA. February 8, 1987.

————. *Jack Longstreet: Last of the Desert Frontiersmen.* Athens, OH: Swallow/ Ohio University Press. 1988.

Index

Books from Nye County Press
by Robert D. McCracken

A History of Amargosa Valley, Nevada (cloth)
ISBN: 1-878138-56-1

The Modern Pioneers of the Amargosa Valley (paper)
ISBN: 1-878138-58-8

A History of Beatty, Nevada (cloth)
ISBN: 1-878138-54-5

Beatty: Frontier Oasis (paper)
ISBN: 1-878138-55-3

A History of Pahrump, Nevada (cloth)
ISBN: 1-878138-51-0

Pahrump: A Valley Waiting to Become a City (paper)
ISBN: 1-878138-53-7

A History of Tonopah, Nevada (cloth)
ISBN: 1-878138-52-9

Tonopah: The Greatest, the Richest, and the Best Mining Town in the World (paper)
ISBN: 1-878138-50-2

Nye County Press
P.O. Box 3070
Tonopah, NV 89049